A TREASURY OF WAR POETRY

ISBN: 1-4264-3200-3

George Herbert Clarke
Professor of English in the University of Tennessee

A TREASURY OF WAR POETRY

THE RIVERSIDE LITERATURE SERIES

BRITISH AND AMERICAN POEMS OF THE WORLD WAR 1914-1917

A TREASURY OF WAR POETRY

CONTENTS

ACKNOWLEDGMENTS

The Editor desires to express his cordial appreciation of the assistance rendered him in his undertaking by the officials of the British Museum (Mr. F.D. Sladen, in particular); Professor W. Macneile Dixon, of the University of Glasgow; Professor Kemp Smith, of Princeton University; Miss Esther C. Johnson, of Needham, Massachusetts; and Mr. Francis Bickley, of London. He wishes also to acknowledge the courtesies generously extended by the following authors, periodicals, and publishers in granting permission for the use of the poems indicated, rights in which are in each case reserved by the owner of the copyright:—

Mr. Francis Bickley and the *Westminster Gazette*:—"The Players."

Mr. F.W. Bourdillon and the *Spectator*:—"The Debt Unpayable."

Dr. Robert Bridges and the London *Times*:—"Lord Kitchener," and "To the United States of America."

Mr. Dana Burnet and the New York *Evening Sun*:—"The Battle of Liège."

Mr. Wilfred Campbell and the Ottawa *Evening Journal*:—"Langemarck at Ypres."

Mr. Patrick R. Chalmers and *Punch*:—"Guns of Verdun."

Mr. Cecil Chesterton and *The New Witness*:—"France."

Mr. Oscar C.A. Child and *Harper's Magazine*:—"To a Hero."

Mr. Reginald McIntosh Cleveland and the *New York Times*:—"Destroyers off Jutland."

Miss Charlotte Holmes Crawford and *Scribner's Magazine*:—"*Vive la France!*"

Mr. Moray Dalton and the *Spectator*:—"Rupert Brooke."

Lord Desborough and the London *Times*:—"Into Battle," by the late Captain Julian Grenfell.

Professor W. Macneile Dixon and the London *Times*:—"To Fellow Travellers in Greece,"

Mr. Austin, Dobson and the *Spectator*:—"'When There Is Peace;'"

Sir Arthur Conan Doyle and the London *Times*:—"The Guards Came Through."

Mr. John Finley and the *Atlantic Monthly*:—"The Road to Dieppe"; Mr. Finley, the American Red Cross, and the *Red Cross Magazine*:—"The Red Cross Spirit Speaks."

Mr. John Freeman and the *Westminster Gazette*:—"The Return."

Mr. Robert Frost and the *Yale Review*:—"Not to Keep."

Mr. John Galsworthy and the *Westminster Gazette*:—"England to Free Men"; Mr. Galsworthy and the London *Chronicle*:—"Russia—America."

Mrs. Theodosia Garrison and *Scribner's Magazine*:—"The Soul of Jeanne d'Arc."

Lady Glenconner and the London *Times*:—"Home Thoughts from Laventie," by the late Lieutenant E. Wyndham Tennant.

Mr. Robert Grant and the *Nation* (New York):—"The Superman."

Mr. Hermann Hagedorn and the *Century Magazine*:—"Resurrection."

Mr. James Norman Hall and the *Spectator*:—"The Cricketers of Flanders."

Mr. Thomas Hardy and the London *Times*:—"Men Who March Away," and "Then and Now."

Mr. John Helston and the *English Review*:—"Kitchener."

Mr. Maurice Hewlett:—"In the Trenches," from *Sing-Songs of the War* (The Poetry Bookshop).

Dr. A. E. Hillard:—"The Dawn Patrol," by Lieutenant Paul Bewsher.

Mrs. Katharine Tynan Hinkson:—"To the Others" and "The Old Soldier."

Mrs. Florence T. Holt and the *Atlantic Monthly*:—"England and America."

Mr. William Dean Howells and the *North American Review*:—"The Passengers of a Retarded Submersible."

Lady Hutchinson:—"Sonnets," by the late Lieutenant Henry William Hutchinson.

Mr. Robert Underwood Johnson:—"To Russia New and Free," from *Poems of War and Peace*, published by the author.

Mr. Rudyard Kipling:—"The Choice"; "'For All we Have and Are'"; and "The Mine-Sweepers." (Copyright, 1914, 1915, 1917, by Rudyard Kipling.)

Captain James H. Knight-Adkin and the *Spectator*;—"No Man's Land" and *"On Les Aura!"*

Sergeant Joseph Lee and the *Spectator*:—"German Prisoners."

Mr. E. V. Lucas and the *Sphere*:—"The Debt."

Mr. Walter de la Mare and the London *Times*:—"'How Sleep the Brave!'"; Mr. de la Mare and the *Westminster Gazette*:—"The Fool Rings his Bells."

Mr. Edward Marsh, literary executor of the late Rupert Brooke:—"The Soldier" and "The Dead."

Mr. Thomas L. Masson:—"The Red Cross Nurses," from the *Red Cross Magazine*.

Lieutenant Charles Langbridge Morgan and the *Westminster Gazette*:—"To America."

Sir Henry Newbolt:—"The Vigil"; "The War Films"; "The Toy Band," and "A Letter from the Front."

Mr. Alfred Noyes:—"Princeton, May, 1917"; "The Searchlights" (London *Times*), "A Prayer in Time of War" (London *Daily Mail*), and "Kilmeny."

Mr. Will H. Ogilvie:—"Canadians."

Mr. Barry Pain and the London *Times*:—"The Kaiser and God."

Miss Marjorie Pickthall and the London *Times*:—"Canada to England."

Canon H.D. Dawnsley and the *Westminster Gazette*:—"At St. Paul's, April 20, 1917."

Dr. Charles Alexander Richmond:—"A Song."

Lieutenant-Colonel Sir Ronald Ross and the *Poetry Review*:—"The Death of Peace."

Mr. Robert Haven Schauffler:—"The White Comrade."

Mr. W. Snow and the *Spectator*:—"Oxford in War-Time."

Mrs. Grace Ellery Channing Stetson and the New York *Tribune*:—*"Qui Vive?"*

Mr. Rowland Thirlmere and the *Poetry Review*:—"Jimmy Doane."

Mrs. Ada Turrell and the *Saturday Review*:—"My Son."

Dr. Henry van Dyke and the London *Times*:—"Liberty Enlightening the World," and *"Mare Liberum"*; Dr. van Dyke and the *Art World*: "The Name of France."

Mr. Tertius van Dyke and the *Spectator*:—"Oxford Revisited in War-Time."

Mrs. Edith Wharton:—"Belgium," from *King Albert's Book* (Hearst's International Library Company).

Mr. George Edward Woodberry and the *Boston Herald*:—"On the Italian Front, MCMXVI"; Mr. Woodberry, the *New York Times* and the *North American Review*:—"Sonnets Written in the Fall of 1914."

The Athenaeum:—"A Cross in Flanders," by G. Rostrevor Hamilton.

The Poetry Review:—"The Messines Road," by Captain J.E. Stewart; "—But a Short Time to Live," by the late Sergeant Leslie Coulson.

The Spectator:—"The Challenge of the Guns," by Private A.N. Field.

The London *Times*:—"To Our Fallen" and "A Petition," by the late Lieutenant Robert Ernest Vernède.

The *Westminster Gazette*:—"Lines Written in Surrey, 1917," by George Herbert Clarke.

Messrs. Barse & Hopkins:—"Fleurette," by Robert W. Service.

The Cambridge University Press and Professor William R. Sorley:—"*Expectans Expectavi*"; "'All the Hills and Vales Along,'" and "Two Sonnets," by the late Captain Charles Hamilton Sorley, from *Marlborough and Other Poems.*

Messrs. Chatto & Windus:—"Fulfilment" and "The Day's March," by Robert Nichols.

Messrs. Constable & Company:—"Pro Patria," "Thomas of the Light Heart," and "To Belgium in Exile," by Sir Owen Seaman, from *War-Time*; "To France" and "*Requiescant*," by Canon and Major Frederick George Scott, from *In the Battle Silences.*

Messrs. E. P. Dutton & Company:—"To a Soldier in Hospital" (the *Spectator*); "Chaplain to the Forces" and "The Spires of Oxford" (*Westminster Gazette*), by Winifred M. Letts, from *Hallowe'en, and Poems of the War*; "A Chant of Love for England," by Helen Gray Cone, from *A Chant of Love for England, and Other Poems* (published also by J.M. Dent & Sons, Limited, London).

Lawrence J. Gomme:—"Italy in Arms," by Clinton Scollard, from *Italy in Arms, and Other Poems.*

Messrs. Houghton Mifflin Company:—"To the Belgians"; "Men of Verdun"; "The Anvil"; "Edith Cavell"; "The Healers" and "For the Fallen," by Laurence Binyon, from *The Cause* (published also by Elkin Mathews, London, in *The Anvil* and *The Winnowing Fan*); "Headquarters," by Captain Gilbert Frankau, from *A Song of the Guns*; "Place de la Concorde" and "In War-Time," by Florence Earle Coates, from *The Collected Poems of Florence Earle Coates*; "Harvest Moon" and "Harvest Moon, 1915," by Josephine Preston Peabody, from *Harvest Moon*; "The Mobilization in Brittany" and "The Journey," by Grace Fallow Norton, from *Roads*, and "Rheims Cathedral—1914," by Grace Hazard Conkling, from *Afternoons of April.*

John Lane:—"The Kaiser and Belgium," by the late Stephen Phillips.

The John Lane Company:—"The Wife of Flanders," by Gilbert K. Chesterton, from *Poems* (published also by Messrs. Burns and Gates, London); "The Soldier," and "The Dead," by the late Lieutenant Rupert Brooke, from *The Collected Poems of Rupert Brooke* (published also by Messrs. Sidgwick & Jackson, London, in *1914, and Other Poems*).

Erskine Macdonald:—The following poems from *Soldier Poets*:—"The Beach Road by the Wood," by Lieutenant Geoffrey Howard; "Before Action," by the late Lieutenant W.N. Hodgson ("Edward Melbourne"); "Courage," by Lieutenant Dyneley Hussey; "Optimism," by Lieutenant A. Victor Ratcliffe; "The Battlefield," by Major Sidney Oswald; "To an Old Lady Seen at a Guest-House for Soldiers," by Corporal Alexander Robertson; "The Casualty Clearing Station," by Lieutenant Gilbert Waterhouse; and "Hills of Home," by Lance-Corporal Malcolm Hemphrey.

The Macmillan Company:—"To Belgium"; "Verdun"; "To a Mother," and "Song of the Red Cross," by Eden Phillpotts, from *Plain Song, 1914-1916* (published also by William Heinemann, London); "The Island of Skyros," by John

Masefield; "Abraham Lincoln Walks at Midnight," from *The Congo and Other Poems*, by Vachel Lindsay; "O Glorious France," by Edgar Lee Masters, from *Songs and Satires*; "Christmas, 1915," from *Poems and Plays*, by Percy MacKaye; "The Hellgate of Soissons," by Herbert Kaufman, from *The Hellgate of Soissons*; "Spring in War-Time," by Sara Teasdale, from *Rivers to the Sea*; and "Retreat," "The Messages," and "Between the Lines," by Wilfrid Wilson Gibson.

Messrs. Macmillan & Company:—"Australia to England," by Archibald T. Strong, from *Sonnets of the Empire*, and "Men Who March Away," by Thomas Hardy, from *Satires of Circumstance.*

Elkin Mathews:—"The British Merchant Service" (the *Spectator*), by C. Fox Smith, from *The Naval Crown.*

John Murray:—"The Sign," and "The Trenches," by Lieutenant Frederic Manning.

The Princeton University Press:—"To France," by Herbert Jones, from *A Book of Princeton Verse.*

Messrs. Charles Scribner's Sons:—"I Have a Rendezvous with Death," and "Champagne, 1914-1915," by the late Alan Seeger, from *Poems.*

Messrs. Sherman, French & Company:—"The *William P. Frye*" *(New York Times)*, by Jeanne Robert Foster, from *Wild Apples.*

Messrs. Sidgwick & Jackson:—"We Willed It Not" *(The Sphere)*, by John Drinkwater; "Three Hills" (London *Times*), by Everard Owen, from *Three Hills, and Other Poems*; "The Volunteer," and "The Fallen Subaltern," by Lieutenant Herbert Asquith, from *The Volunteer, and Other Poems.*

Messrs. Truslove and Hanson:—"A Mother's Dedication," by Margaret Peterson, from *The Women's Message.*

INTRODUCTION

Because man is both militant and pacific, he has expressed in literature, as indeed in the other forms of art, his pacific and militant moods. Nor are these moods, of necessity, incompatible. War may become the price of peace, and peace may so decay as inevitably to bring about war. Of the dully unresponsive pacificist and the jingo patriot, quick to anger, the latter no doubt is the more dangerous to the cause of true freedom, yet both are "undesirable citizens." He who believes that peace is illusory and spurious, unless it be based upon justice and liberty, will be proud to battle, if battle he must, for the sake of those foundations.

For the most part, the poetry of war, undertaken in this spirit, has touched and exalted such special qualities as patriotism, courage, self-sacrifice, enterprise, and endurance. Where it has tended to glorify war in itself, it is chiefly because war has released those qualities, so to speak, in stirring and spectacular ways; and where it has chosen to round upon war and to upbraid it, it is because war has slain ardent and lovable youths and has brought misery and despair to women and old people. But the war poet has left the mere arguments to others. For himself, he has seen and felt. Envisaging war from various angles, now romantically, now realistically, now as the celebrating chronicler, now as the contemplative interpreter, but always in a spirit of catholic curiosity, he has sung, the fall of Troy, the Roman adventures, the mediaeval battles and crusades, the fields of Agincourt and Waterloo, and the more modern revolutions. Since Homer, he has spoken with martial eloquence through, the voices of Drayton, Spenser, Marlowe, Webster, Shakespeare, Milton, Byron, Scott, Burns, Campbell, Tennyson, Browning, the New England group, and Walt Whitman,—to mention only a few of the British and American names,—and he speaks sincerely and powerfully to-day in the writings of Kipling. Hardy, Masefield, Binyon, Newbolt,

Watson, Rupert Brooke, and the two young soldiers—the one English, the other American—who have lately lost their lives while on active service: Captain Charles Hamilton Sorley, who was killed at Hulluch, October 18, 1915; and Alan Seeger, who fell, mortally wounded, during the charge on Belloy-en-Santerre, July 4, 1916.

There can be little doubt that these several minds and spirits, stirred by the passion and energy of war, and reacting sensitively both to its cruelties and to its pities, have experienced the kinship of quickened insight and finer unselfishness in the face of wide-ranging death. They have silently compared, perhaps, the normal materialistic conventions in business, politics, education, and religion, with the relief from those conventions that nearly all soldiers and many civilians experience in time of war; for although war has its too gross and ugly side, it has not dared to learn that inflexibility of custom and conduct that deadens the spirit into a tame submission. This strange rebound and exaltation would seem to be due less to the physical realities of war—which must in many ways cramp and constrain the individual—than to the relative spiritual freedom engendered by the needs of war, if they are to be successfully met. The man of war has an altogether unusual opportunity to realize himself, to cleanse and heal himself through the mastering of his physical fears; through the facing of his moral doubts; through the reëxamination of whatever thoughts he may have possessed, theretofore, about life and death and the universe; and through the quietly unselfish devotion he owes to the welfare of his fellows and to the cause of his native land.

Into the stuff of his thought and utterance, whether he be on active service or not, the poet-interpreter of war weaves these intentions, and coöperates with his fellows in building up a little higher and better, from time to time, that edifice of truth for whose completion can be spared no human experience, no human hope.

As already suggested, English and American literatures have both received genuine accessions, even thus early, arising out of the present great conflict, and we may be sure that other equally notable contributions will be made. The present Anthology contains a number of representative poems produced by English-speaking men and women. The editorial policy has been humanly hospitable, rather than academically critical, especially in the case of some of the verses written by soldiers at the Front, which, however slight in certain instances their technical merit may be, are yet psychologically interesting as sincere transcripts of personal experience, and will, it is thought, for that very reason, peculiarly attract and interest the reader. It goes without saying that there are several poems in this group which conspicuously succeed also as works of art. For the rest, the attempt has been made, within such limitations as have been experienced, to present pretty freely the best of what has been found available in contemporary British and American war verse. It must speak for itself, and the reader will find that in not a few instances it does so with sensitive sympathy and with living power; sometimes, too, with that quietly intimate companionableness which we find in Gray's *Elegy*, and which John Masefield, while lecturing in America in 1916, so often indicated as a prime quality in English poetry. But if this quality appears in Chaucer and the pre-Romantics and Wordsworth, it appears also in Longfellow and Lowell, in Emerson and Lanier, and in William Vaughn Moody; for American poetry is, after all, as English poetry,—"with a difference,"—sprung from the same sources, and coursing along similar channels.

The new fellowship of the two great Anglo-Saxon nations which a book of this character may, to a degree, illustrate, is filled with such high promise for both of them, and for all civilization, that it is perhaps hardly too much to say, with Ambassador Walter H. Page, in his address at the Pilgrims' Dinner in London, April 12, 1917: "We shall get out of this association an indissoluble companionship, and we shall henceforth have indissoluble mutual duties for mankind. I doubt if there could be another international event comparable in large value and in long consequences to this closer association." Mr. Balfour struck the same note when, during his mission to the United States, he expressed himself in these words: "That this great people should throw themselves whole-heartedly into this mighty struggle, prepared for all efforts and sacrifices that may be required to win success for this most righteous cause, is an event at once so happy and so momentous that only the historian of the future will be able, as I believe, to measure its true proportions."

The words of these eminent men ratify in the field of international politics the hopeful anticipation which Tennyson expressed in his poem, *Hands all Round*, as it appeared in the London *Examiner*, February 7, 1852:—

"Gigantic daughter of the West,
    We drink to thee across the flood,
We know thee most, we love thee best,
    For art thou not of British blood?
Should war's mad blast again be blown,
    Permit not thou the tyrant powers
To fight thy mother here alone,
    But let thy broadsides roar with ours.
            Hands all round!
    God the tyrant's cause confound!
To our great kinsmen of the West, my friends,
    And the great name of England, round and round.

"O rise, our strong Atlantic sons,
    When war against our freedom springs!
O speak to Europe through your guns!
    They can be understood by kings.
You must not mix our Queen with those
    That wish to keep their people fools;
Our freedom's foemen are her foes,
    She comprehends the race she rules.
            Hands all round!
    God the tyrant's cause confound!
To our dear kinsmen of the West, my friends,
    And the great cause of Freedom, round and round."

They ratify also the spirit of those poems in the present volume which seek to interpret to Britons and Americans their deepening friendship. "Poets," said Shelley, "are the unacknowledged legislators of the world," and he meant by legislation the guidance and determination of the verdicts of the human soul.

G. H. C.
August, 1917

THE CHOICE

THE AMERICAN SPIRIT SPEAKS:

To the Judge of Right and Wrong
  With Whom fulfillment lies
Our purpose and our power belong,
  Our faith and sacrifice.

Let Freedom's land rejoice!
  Our ancient bonds are riven;
Once more to us the eternal choice
  Of good or ill is given.

Not at a little cost,
  Hardly by prayer or tears,
Shall we recover the road we lost
  In the drugged and doubting years,

But after the fires and the wrath,
  But after searching and pain,
His Mercy opens us a path
  To live with ourselves again.

In the Gates of Death rejoice!
  We see and hold the good—
Bear witness, Earth, we have made our choice
  For Freedom's brotherhood.

Then praise the Lord Most High
  Whose Strength hath saved us whole,

Who bade us choose that the Flesh should die
    And not the living Soul!

Rudyard Kipling

"LIBERTY ENLIGHTENING THE WORLD"

Thou warden of the western gate, above Manhattan Bay,
The fogs of doubt that hid thy face are driven clean away:
Thine eyes at last look far and clear, thou liftest high thy hand
To spread the light of liberty world-wide for every land.

No more thou dreamest of a peace reserved alone for thee,
While friends are fighting for thy cause beyond the guardian sea:
The battle that they wage is thine; thou fallest if they fall;
The swollen flood of Prussian pride will sweep unchecked
    o'er all.

O cruel is the conquer-lust in Hohenzollern brains:
The paths they plot to gain their goal are dark with shameful
    stains:
No faith they keep, no law revere, no god but naked Might;—
They are the foemen of mankind. Up, Liberty, and smite!

Britain, and France, and Italy, and Russia newly born,
Have waited for thee in the night. Oh, come as comes the
    morn.
Serene and strong and full of faith, America, arise,
With steady hope and mighty help to join thy brave Allies.

O dearest country of my heart, home of the high desire,
Make clean thy soul for sacrifice on Freedom's altar-fire:
For thou must suffer, thou must fight, until the warlords
    cease,
And all the peoples lift their heads in liberty and peace.

Henry van Dyke
April 10, 1917

TO THE UNITED STATES OF AMERICA

Brothers in blood! They who this wrong began
    To wreck our commonwealth, will rue the day
    When first they challenged freemen to the fray,
And with the Briton dared the American.
Now are we pledged to win the Rights of man;
    Labour and Justice now shall have their way,
    And in a League of Peace—God grant we may—
Transform the earth, not patch up the old plan.

Sure is our hope since he who led your nation
    Spake for mankind, and ye arose in awe
Of that high call to work the world's salvation;
        Clearing your minds of all estranging blindness
    In the vision of Beauty and the Spirit's law,
        Freedom and Honour and sweet Lovingkindness.

Robert Bridges
April 30, 1917

ABRAHAM LINCOLN WALKS AT MIDNIGHT

(IN SPRINGFIELD, ILLINOIS)

It is portentous, and a thing of state
That here at midnight, in our little town,
A mourning figure walks, and will not rest,
Near the old court-house pacing up and down,

Or by his homestead, or in shadowed yards
He lingers where his children used to play;
Or through the market, on the well-worn stones
He stalks until the dawn-stars burn away.

A bronzed, lank man! His suit of ancient black,
A famous high top-hat and plain worn shawl
Make him the quaint great figure that men love,
The prairie-lawyer, master of us all.

He cannot sleep upon his hillside now.
He is among us:—as in times before!
And we who toss and lie awake for long
Breathe deep, and start, to see him pass the door.

His head is bowed. He thinks on men and kings.
Yea, when the sick world cries, how can he sleep?
Too many peasants fight, they know not why,
Too many homesteads in black terror weep.

The sins of all the war-lords burn his heart.
He sees the dreadnaughts scouring every main.
He carries on his shawl-wrapped shoulders now
The bitterness, the folly, and the pain.

He cannot rest until a spirit-dawn
Shall come;—the shining hope of Europe free:
The league of sober folk, the Workers' Earth
Bringing long peace to Cornland, Alp, and Sea.

It breaks his heart that kings must murder still,
That all his hours of travail here for men
Seem yet in vain. And who will bring white peace
That he may sleep upon his hill again?

Vachel Lindsay

THE "WILLIAM P. FRYE"

I saw her first abreast the Boston Light
At anchor; she had just come in, turned head,
And sent her hawsers creaking, clattering down.
I was so near to where the hawse-pipes fed
The cable out from her careening bow,
I moved up on the swell, shut steam and lay
Hove to in my old launch to look at her.
She'd come in light, a-skimming up the Bay
Like a white ghost with topsails bellying full;
And all her noble lines from bow to stern

Made music in the wind; it seemed she rode
The morning air like those thin clouds that turn
Into tall ships when sunrise lifts the clouds
From calm sea-courses.

There, in smoke-smudged coats,
Lay funnelled liners, dirty fishing-craft,
Blunt cargo-luggers, tugs, and ferry-boats.
Oh, it was good in that black-scuttled lot
To see the *Frye* come lording on her way
Like some old queen that we had half forgot
Come to her own. A little up the Bay
The Fort lay green, for it was springtime then;
The wind was fresh, rich with the spicy bloom
Of the New England coast that tardily
Escapes, late April, from an icy tomb.
The State-house glittered on old Beacon Hill,
Gold in the sun . . . 'T was all so fair awhile;
But she was fairest—this great square-rigged ship
That had blown in from some far happy isle
On from the shores of the Hesperides.

They caught her in a South Atlantic road
Becalmed, and found her hold brimmed up with wheat;
"Wheat's contraband," they said, and blew her hull
To pieces, murdered one of our staunch fleet,
Fast dwindling, of the big old sailing ships
That carry trade for us on the high sea
And warped out of each harbor in the States.
It wasn't law, so it seems strange to me—
A big mistake. Her keel's struck bottom now
And her four masts sunk fathoms, fathoms deep
To Davy Jones. The dank seaweed will root
On her oozed decks, and the cross-surges sweep
Through the set sails; but never, never more
Her crew will stand away to brace and trim,
Nor sea-blown petrels meet her thrashing up
To windward on the Gulf Stream's stormy rim;
Never again she'll head a no'theast gale

Or like a spirit loom up, sliding dumb,
And ride in safe beyond the Boston Light,
To make the harbor glad because she's come.

Jeanne Robert Foster

ENGLAND AND AMERICA

Mother and child! Though the dividing sea
  Shall roll its tide between us, we are one,
  Knit by immortal memories, and none
But feels the throb of ancient fealty.
A century has passed since at thy knee
  We learnt the speech of freemen, caught the fire
  That would not brook thy menaces, when sire
And grandsire hurled injustice back to thee.

But the full years have wrought equality:
  The past outworn, shall not the future bring
  A deeper union, from whose life shall spring
Mankind's best hope? In the dark night of strife
Men perished for their dream of Liberty
Whose lives were given for this larger life.

Florence T. Holt

TO AMERICA

When the fire sinks in the grate, and night has bent
Close wings about the room, and winter stands
Hard-eyed before the window, when the hands
Have turned the book's last page and friends are sleeping,
Thought, as it were an old stringed instrument
Drawn to remembered music, oft does set
The lips moving in prayer, for us fresh keeping
Knowledge of springtime and the violet.

And, as the eyes grow dim with many years,
The spirit runs more swiftly than the feet,

Perceives its comfort, knows that it will meet
God at the end of troubles, that the dreary
Last reaches of old age lead beyond tears
To happy youth unending. There is peace
In homeward waters, where at last the weary
Shall find rebirth, and their long struggle cease.

So, at this hour, when the Old World lies sick,
Beyond the pain, the agony of breath
Hard drawn, beyond the menaces of death,
O'er graves and years leans out the eager spirit.
First must the ancient die; then shall be quick
New fires within us. Brother, we shall make
Incredible discoveries and inherit
The fruits of hope, and love shall be awake.

Charles Langbridge Morgan

A CHANT OF LOVE FOR ENGLAND

A song of hate is a song of Hell;
Some there be that sing it well.
Let them sing it loud and long,
We lift our hearts in a loftier song:
We lift our hearts to Heaven above,
Singing the glory of her we love,—
England!

Glory of thought and glory of deed,
Glory of Hampden and Runnymede;
Glory of ships that sought far goals,
Glory of swords and glory of souls!
Glory of songs mounting as birds,
Glory immortal of magical words;
Glory of Milton, glory of Nelson,
Tragical glory of Gordon and Scott;
Glory of Shelley, glory of Sidney,
Glory transcendent that perishes not,—

Hers is the story, hers be the glory,
England!

Shatter her beauteous breast ye may;
The spirit of England none can slay!
Dash the bomb on the dome of Paul's—
Deem ye the fame of the Admiral falls?
Pry the stone from the chancel floor,—
Dream ye that Shakespeare shall live no more?
Where is the giant shot that kills
Wordsworth walking the old green hills?
Trample the red rose on the ground,—
Keats is Beauty while earth spins round!
Bind her, grind her, burn her with fire,
Cast her ashes into the sea,—
She shall escape, she shall aspire,
She shall arise to make men free:
She shall arise in a sacred scorn,
Lighting the lives that are yet unborn;
Spirit supernal, Splendour eternal,
ENGLAND!

Helen Gray Cone

AT ST. PAUL'S

APRIL 20, 1917

Not since Wren's Dome has whispered with man's prayer
Have angels leaned to wonder out of Heaven
At such uprush of intercession given,
Here where to-day one soul two nations share,
And with accord send up thro' trembling air
Their vows to strive as Honour ne'er has striven
Till back to hell the Lords of hell are driven,
And Life and Peace again shall flourish fair.

This is the day of conscience high-enthroned,
The day when East is West and West is East

To strike for human Love and Freedom's word
Against foul wrong that cannot be atoned;
To-day is hope of brotherhood's bond increased,
And Christ, not Odin, is acclaimed the Lord.

Hardwicke Drummond Rawnsley

JIMMY DOANE

Often I think of you, Jimmy Doane,—
You who, light-heartedly, came to my house
Three autumns, to shoot and to eat a grouse!

As I sat apart in this quiet room,
My mind was full of the horror of war
And not with the hope of a visitor.

I had dined on food that had lost its taste;
My soul was cold and I wished you were here,—
When, all in a moment, I knew you were near.

Placing that chair where you used to sit,
I looked at my book:—Three years to-day
Since you laughed in that seat and I heard you say—

"My country is with you, whatever befall:
America—Britain—these two are akin
In courage and honour; they underpin

"The rights of Mankind!" Then you grasped my hand
With a brotherly grip, and you made me feel
Something that Time would surely reveal.

You were comely and tall; you had corded arms,
And sympathy's grace with your strength was blent;
You were generous, clever, and confident.

There was that in your hopes which uncountable lives
Have perished to make; your heart was fulfilled
With the breath of God that can never be stilled.

A living symbol of power, you talked
Of the work to do in the world to make
Life beautiful: yes, and my heartstrings ache

To think how you, at the stroke of War,
Chose that your steadfast soul should fly
With the eagles of France as their proud ally.

You were America's self, dear lad—
The first swift son of your bright, free land
To heed the call of the Inner Command—

To image its spirit in such rare deeds
As braced the valour of France, who knows
That the heart of America thrills with her woes.

For a little leaven leavens the whole!
Mostly we find, when we trouble to seek
The soul of a people, that some unique,

Brave man is its flower and symbol, who
Makes bold to utter the words that choke
The throats of feebler, timider folk.

You flew for the western eagle—and fell
Doing great things for your country's pride:
For the beauty and peace of life you died.

Britain and France have shrined in their souls
Your memory; yes, and for ever you share
Their love with their perished lords of the air.

Invisible now, in that empty seat,
You sit, who came through the clouds to me,
Swift as a message from over the sea.

My house is always open to you:
Dear spirit, come often and you will find
Welcome, where mind can foregather with mind!

And may we sit together one day
Quietly here, when a word is said
To bring new gladness unto our dead,

Knowing your dream is a dream no more;
And seeing on some momentous pact
Your vision upbuilt as a deathless fact.

Rowland Thirlmere

PRINCETON, MAY, 1917

Here Freedom stood by slaughtered friend and foe,
And, ere the wrath paled or that sunset died,
Looked through the ages; then, with eyes aglow,
Laid them to wait that future, side by side.

(Lines for a monument to the American and British soldiers of the Revolutionary War who fell on the Princeton battlefield and were buried in one grave.)

Now lamp-lit gardens in the blue dusk shine
  Through dogwood, red and white;
And round the gray quadrangles, line by line,
  The windows fill with light,
Where Princeton calls to Magdalen, tower to tower,
  Twin lanthorns of the law;
And those cream-white magnolia boughs embower
  The halls of "Old Nassau."

The dark bronze tigers crouch on either side
  Where redcoats used to pass;
And round the bird-loved house where Mercer died,
  And violets dusk the grass,
By Stony Brook that ran so red of old,

But sings of friendship now,
To feed the old enemy's harvest fifty-fold
The green earth takes the plow.

Through this May night, if one great ghost should stray
With deep remembering eyes,
Where that old meadow of battle smiles away
Its blood-stained memories,
If Washington should walk, where friend and foe
Sleep and forget the past,
Be sure his unquenched heart would leap to know
Their souls are linked at last.

Be sure he waits, in shadowy buff and blue,
Where those dim lilacs wave.
He bends his head to bless, as dreams come true,
The promise of that grave;
Then, with a vaster hope than thought can scan,
Touching his ancient sword,
Prays for that mightier realm of God in man:
"Hasten thy kingdom, Lord.

"Land of our hope, land of the singing stars,
Type of the world to be,
The vision of a world set free from wars
Takes life, takes form from thee;
Where all the jarring nations of this earth,
Beneath the all-blessing sun,
Bring the new music of mankind to birth,
And make the whole world one."

And those old comrades rise around him there,
Old foemen, side by side,
With eyes like stars upon the brave night air,
And young as when they died,
To hear your bells, O beautiful Princeton towers,
Ring for the world's release.

They see you piercing like gray swords through flowers,
  And smile, from souls at peace.

Alfred Noyes

THE VIGIL

England! where the sacred flame
    Burns before the inmost shrine,
Where the lips that love thy name
    Consecrate their hopes and thine,
Where the banners of thy dead
Weave their shadows overhead,
Watch beside thine arms to-night,
Pray that God defend the Right.

Think that when to-morrow comes
    War shall claim command of all,
Thou must hear the roll of drums,
    Thou must hear the trumpet's call.
Now, before thy silence ruth,
Commune with the voice of truth;
England! on thy knees to-night
Pray that God defend the Right.

Single-hearted, unafraid,
    Hither all thy heroes came,
On this altar's steps were laid
    Gordon's life and Outram's fame.
England! if thy will be yet
By their great example set,
Here beside thine arms to-night
Pray that God defend the Right.

So shalt thou when morning comes
    Rise to conquer or to fall,
Joyful hear the rolling drums,
    Joyful tear the trumpets call,
Then let Memory tell thy heart:

"England! what thou wert, thou art!"
Gird thee with thine ancient might,
Forth! and God defend the Right!

Henry Newbolt

"FOR ALL WE HAVE AND ARE"

For all we have and are,
For all our children's fate,
Stand up and meet the war.
The Hun is at the gate!
Our world has passed away
In wantonness o'erthrown.
There is nothing left to-day
But steel and fire and stone.

Though all we knew depart,
The old commandments stand:
"In courage keep your heart,
In strength lift up your hand,"

Once more we hear the word
That sickened earth of old:
"No law except the sword
Unsheathed and uncontrolled,"
Once more it knits mankind.
Once more the nations go
To meet and break and bind
A crazed and driven foe.
Comfort, content, delight—
The ages' slow-bought gain—
They shrivelled in a night,
Only ourselves remain
To face the naked days
In silent fortitude,
Through perils and dismays
Renewed and re-renewed.

Though all we made depart,
The old commandments stand:
"In patience keep your heart,
In strength lift up your hand."

No easy hopes or lies
Shall bring us to our goal,
But iron sacrifice
Of body, will, and soul
There is but one task for all—
For each one life to give.
Who stands if freedom fall?
Who dies if England live?

Rudyard Kipling

ENGLAND TO FREE MEN

Men of my blood, you English men!
From misty hill and misty fen,
From cot, and town, and plough, and moor,
Come in—before I shut the door!
Into my courtyard paved with stones
That keep the names, that keep the bones,
Of none but English men who came
Free of their lives, to guard my fame.

I am your native land who bred
No driven heart, no driven head;
I fly a flag in every sea
Round the old Earth, of Liberty!
I am the Land that boasts a crown;
The sun comes up, the sun goes down—
And never men may say of me,
Mine is a breed that is not free.

I have a wreath! My forehead wears
A hundred leaves—a hundred years
I never knew the words: "You must!"

And shall my wreath return to dust?
Freemen! The door is yet ajar;
From northern star to southern star,
O ye who count and ye who delve,
Come in—before my clock strikes twelve!

John Galsworthy

PRO PATRIA

England, in this great fight to which you go
Because, where Honour calls you, go you must,
Be glad, whatever comes, at least to know
You have your quarrel just.

Peace was your care; before the nations' bar
Her cause you pleaded and her ends you sought;
But not for her sake, being what you are,
Could you be bribed and bought.

Others may spurn the pledge of land to land,
May with the brute sword stain a gallant past;
But by the seal to which *you* set your hand,
Thank God, you still stand fast!

Forth, then, to front that peril of the deep
With smiling lips and in your eyes the light,
Steadfast and confident, of those who keep
Their storied 'scutcheon bright.

And we, whose burden is to watch and wait,—
High-hearted ever, strong in faith and prayer,—
We ask what offering we may consecrate,
What humble service share.

To steel our souls against the lust of ease;
To bear in silence though our hearts may bleed;
To spend ourselves, and never count the cost,
For others' greater need;—

To go our quiet ways, subdued and sane;
To hush all vulgar clamour of the street;
With level calm to face alike the strain
Of triumph or defeat;

This be our part, for so we serve you best,
So best confirm their prowess and their pride,
Your warrior sons, to whom in this high test
Our fortunes we confide.

Owen Seaman
August 12, 1914

LINES WRITTEN IN SURREY, 1917

A sudden swirl of song in the bright sky—
The little lark adoring his lord the sun;
Across the corn the lazy ripples run;
Under the eaves, conferring drowsily,

Doves droop or amble; the agile waterfly
Wrinkles the pool; and flowers, gay and dun,
Rose, bluebell, rhododendron, one by one,
The buccaneering bees prove busily.

Ah, who may trace this tranquil loveliness
In verse felicitous?—no measure tells;
But gazing on her bosom we can guess
Why men strike hard for England in red hells,
Falling on dreams, 'mid Death's extreme caress,
Of English daisies dancing in English dells.

George Herbert Clarke

FRANCE

Because for once the sword broke in her hand,
The words she spoke seemed perished for a space;
All wrong was brazen, and in every land
The tyrants walked abroad with naked face.

The waters turned to blood, as rose the Star
Of evil Fate denying all release.
The rulers smote, the feeble crying "War!"
The usurers robbed, the naked crying "Peace!"

And her own feet were caught in nets of gold,
And her own soul profaned by sects that squirm,
And little men climbed her high seats and sold
Her honour to the vulture and the worm.

And she seemed broken and they thought her dead,
The Overmen, so brave against the weak.
Has your last word of sophistry been said,
O cult of slaves? Then it is hers to speak.

Clear the slow mists from her half-darkened eyes,
As slow mists parted over Valmy fell,
As once again her hands in high surprise
Take hold upon the battlements of Hell.

Cecil Chesterton

THE NAME OF FRANCE

Give us a name to fill the mind
With the shining thoughts that lead mankind,
The glory of learning, the joy of art,—
A name that tells of a splendid part
In the long, long toil and the strenuous fight
Of the human race to win its way
From the feudal darkness into the day
Of Freedom, Brotherhood, Equal Right,—

A name like a star, a name of light—
I give you *France!*

Give us a name to stir the blood
With a warmer glow and a swifter flood,—
A name like the sound of a trumpet, clear,
And silver-sweet, and iron-strong,
That calls three million men to their feet,
Ready to march, and steady to meet
The foes who threaten that name with wrong,—
A name that rings like a battle-song.
I give you *France!*

Give us a name to move the heart
With the strength that noble griefs impart,
A name that speaks of the blood outpoured
To save mankind from the sway of the sword,—
A name that calls on the world to share
In the burden of sacrificial strife
Where the cause at stake is the world's free life
And the rule of the people everywhere,—
A name like a vow, a name like a prayer.
I give you *France!*

Henry van Dyke

VIVE LA FRANCE!

Franceline rose in the dawning gray,
And her heart would dance though she knelt to pray,
For her man Michel had holiday,
Fighting for France.

She offered her prayer by the cradle-side,
And with baby palms folded in hers she cried:
"If I have but one prayer, dear, crucified
Christ—save France!

"But if I have two, then, by Mary's grace,
Carry me safe to the meeting-place,
Let me look once again on my dear love's face,
Save him for France!"

She crooned to her boy: "Oh, how glad he'll be,
Little three-months old, to set eyes on thee!
For, 'Rather than gold, would I give,' wrote he,
'A son to France.'

"Come, now, be good, little stray *sauterelle*,
For we're going by-by to thy papa Michel,
But I'll not say where for fear thou wilt tell,
Little pigeon of France!

"Six days' leave and a year between!
But what would you have? In six days clean,
Heaven was made," said Franceline,
"Heaven and France."

She came to the town of the nameless name,
To the marching troops in the street she came,
And she held high her boy like a taper flame
Burning for France.

Fresh from the trenches and gray with grime,
Silent they march like a pantomime;
"But what need of music? My heart beats time—
Vive la France!"

His regiment comes. Oh, then where is he?
"There is dust in my eyes, for I cannot see,—
Is that my Michel to the right of thee,
Soldier of France?"

Then out of the ranks a comrade fell,—
"Yesterday—'t was a splinter of shell—
And he whispered thy name, did thy poor Michel,
Dying for France."

The tread of the troops on the pavement throbbed
Like a woman's heart of its last joy robbed,
As she lifted her boy to the flag, and sobbed:
"Vive la France!"

Charlotte Holmes Crawford

THE SOUL OF JEANNE D'ARC

She came not into the Presence as a martyred saint might come,
Crowned, white-robed and adoring, with very reverence dumb,—

She stood as a straight young soldier, confident, gallant, strong,
Who asks a boon of his captain in the sudden hush of the drum.

She said: "Now have I stayed too long in this my place of bliss,
With these glad dead that, comforted, forget what sorrow is
Upon that world whose stony stairs they climbed to come to this.

"But lo, a cry hath torn the peace wherein so long I stayed,
Like a trumpet's call at Heaven's wall from a herald unafraid,—
A million voices in one cry, *'Where is the Maid, the Maid?'*

"I had forgot from too much joy that olden task of mine,
But I have heard a certain word shatter the chant divine,
Have watched a banner glow and grow before mine eyes for sign.

"I would return to that my land flung in the teeth of war,
I would cast down my robe and crown that pleasure me no more,
And don the armor that I knew, the valiant sword I bore.

"And angels militant shall fling the gates of Heaven wide,
And souls new-dead whose lives were shed like leaves on war's red tide
Shall cross their swords above our heads and cheer us as we ride,

"For with me goes that soldier saint, Saint Michael of the sword,
And I shall ride on his right side, a page beside his lord,
And men shall follow like swift blades to reap a sure reward.

"Grant that I answer this my call, yea, though the end may be
The naked shame, the biting flame, the last, long agony;
I would go singing down that road where fagots wait for me.

"Mine be the fire about my feet, the smoke above my head;
So might I glow, a torch to show the path my heroes tread;
My Captain! Oh, my Captain, let me go back!" she said.

Theodosia Garrison

O GLORIOUS FRANCE

You have become a forge of snow-white fire,
A crucible of molten steel, O France!
Your sons are stars who cluster to a dawn
And fade in light for you, O glorious France!
They pass through meteor changes with a song
Which to all islands and all continents
Says life is neither comfort, wealth, nor fame,
Nor quiet hearthstones, friendship, wife nor child,
Nor love, nor youth's delight, nor manhood's power,
Nor many days spent in a chosen work,
Nor honored merit, nor the patterned theme
Of daily labor, nor the crowns nor wreaths
Of seventy years.

These are not all of life,
O France, whose sons amid the rolling thunder

Of cannon stand in trenches where the dead
Clog the ensanguined ice. But life to these
Prophetic and enraptured souls is vision,
And the keen ecstasy of fated strife,
And divination of the loss as gain,
And reading mysteries with brightened eyes
In fiery shock and dazzling pain before
The orient splendour of the face of Death,
As a great light beside a shadowy sea;
And in a high will's strenuous exercise,
Where the warmed spirit finds its fullest strength
And is no more afraid, and in the stroke
Of azure lightning when the hidden essence
And shifting meaning of man's spiritual worth
And mystical significance in time
Are instantly distilled to one clear drop
Which mirrors earth and heaven.

This is life
Flaming to heaven in a minute's span
When the breath of battle blows the smouldering spark.
And across these seas
We who cry Peace and treasure life and cling
To cities, happiness, or daily toil
For daily bread, or trail the long routine
Of seventy years, taste not the terrible wine
Whereof you drink, who drain and toss the cup
Empty and ringing by the finished feast;
Or have it shaken from your hand by sight
Of God against the olive woods.

As Joan of Arc amid the apple trees
With sacred joy first heard the voices, then
Obeying plunged at Orleans in a field
Of spears and lived her dream and died in fire,
Thou, France, hast heard the voices and hast lived
The dream and known the meaning of the dream,

And read its riddle: how the soul of man
May to one greatest purpose make itself
A lens of clearness, how it loves the cup
Of deepest truth, and how its bitterest gall
Turns sweet to soul's surrender.

And you say:
Take days for repetition, stretch your hands
For mocked renewal of familiar things:
The beaten path, the chair beside the window,
The crowded street, the task, the accustomed sleep,
And waking to the task, or many springs
Of lifted cloud, blue water, flowering fields—
The prison-house grows close no less, the feast
A place of memory sick for senses dulled
Down to the dusty end where pitiful Time
Grown weary cries Enough!

Edgar Lee Masters

TO FRANCE

Those who have stood for thy cause when the dark was
around thee,
Those who have pierced through the shadows and shining
have found thee,
Those who have held to their faith in thy courage and power,
Thy spirit, thy honor, thy strength for a terrible hour,
Now can rejoice that they see thee in light and in glory,
Facing whatever may come as an end to the story
In calm undespairing, with steady eyes fixed on the
morrow—
The morn that is pregnant with blood and with death and
with sorrow.
And whether the victory crowns thee, O France the eternal,
Or whether the smoke and the dusk of a nightfall infernal
Gather about thee, and us, and the foe; and all treasures

Run with the flooding of war into bottomless measures—
Fall what befalls: in this hour all those who are near thee
And all who have loved thee, they rise and salute and revere
thee!

Herbert Jones

PLACE DE LA CONCORDE

AUGUST 14, 1914

[Since the bombardment of Strasburg, August 14, 1870, her statue in Paris, representing Alsace, has been draped in mourning by the French people.]

Near where the royal victims fell
In days gone by, caught in the swell
Of a ruthless tide
Of human passion, deep and wide:
There where we two
A Nation's later sorrow knew—
To-day, O friend! I stood
Amid a self-ruled multitude
That by nor sound nor word
Betrayed how mightily its heart was stirred,

A memory Time never could efface—
A memory of Grief—
Like a great Silence brooded o'er the place;
And men breathed hard, as seeking for relief
From an emotion strong
That would not cry, though held in check too long.

One felt that joy drew near—
A joy intense that seemed itself to fear—
Brightening in eyes that had been dull,
As all with feeling gazed

Upon the Strasburg figure, raised
Above us—mourning, beautiful!

Then one stood at the statue's base, and spoke—
Men needed not to ask what word;
Each in his breast the message heard,
Writ for him by Despair,
That evermore in moving phrase
Breathes from the Invalides and Père Lachaise—
Vainly it seemed, alas!
But now, France looking on the image there,
Hope gave her back the lost Alsace.

A deeper hush fell on the crowd:
A sound—the lightest—seemed too loud
(Would, friend, you had been there!)
As to that form the speaker rose,
Took from her, fold on fold,
The mournful crape, gray-worn and old,
Her, proudly, to disclose,
And with the touch of tender care
That fond emotion speaks,
'Mid tears that none could quite command,
Placed the Tricolor in her hand,
And kissed her on both cheeks!

Florence Earle Coates

TO FRANCE

What is the gift we have given thee, Sister?
What is the trust we have laid in thy hand?
Hearts of our bravest, our best, and our dearest,
Blood of our blood we have sown in thy land.

What for all time will the harvest be, Sister?
What will spring up from the seed that is sown?

Freedom and peace and goodwill among Nations,
   Love that will bind us with love all our own.

Bright is the path, that is opening before us,
   Upward and onward it mounts through the night;
Sword shall not sever the bonds that unite us
   Leading the world to the fullness of light.

Sorrow hath made thee more beautiful, Sister,
   Nobler and purer than ever before;
We who are chastened by sorrow and anguish
   Hail thee as sister and queen evermore.

Frederick George Scott

QUI VIVE?

Qui vive? Who passes by up there?
Who moves—what stirs in the startled air?
What whispers, thrills, exults up there?
Qui vive?
                    "The Flags of France."

What wind on a windless night is this,
That breathes as light as a lover's kiss,
That blows through the night with bugle notes,
That streams like a pennant from a lance,
That rustles, that floats?
                    "The Flags of France."

What richly moves, what lightly stirs,
Like a noble lady in a dance,
When all men's eyes are in love with hers
And needs must follow?
                    "The Flags of France."

What calls to the heart—and the heart has heard,
Speaks, and the soul has obeyed the word,
Summons, and all the years advance,

And the world goes forward with France—with France?
Who called?
"The Flags of France."

What flies—a glory, through the night,
While the legions stream—a line of light,
And men fall to the left and fall to the right,
But *they* fall not?
"The Flags of France."

Qui vive? Who comes? What approaches there?
What soundless tumult, what breath in the air
Takes the breath in the throat, the blood from the heart?
In a flame of dark, to the unheard beat
Of an unseen drum and fleshless feet,
Without glint of barrel or bayonets' glance,
They approach—they come. *Who* comes? (Hush! Hark!)
"Qui vive?"
"The Flags of France."

Uncover the head and kneel—kneel down,
A monarch passes, without a crown,
Let the proud tears fall but the heart beat high:
The Greatest of All is passing by,
On its endless march in the endless Plan:
"Qui vive?"
"The Spirit of Man."

"O Spirit of Man, pass on! Advance!"
And they who lead, who hold the van?
Kneel down!
The Flags of France.

Grace Ellery Channing
Paris, 1917

TO THE BELGIANS

O Race that Caesar knew,
That won stern Roman praise,
What land not envies you
The laurel of these days?

You built your cities rich
Around each towered hall,—
Without, the statued niche,
Within, the pictured wall.

Your ship-thronged wharves; your marts
With gorgeous Venice vied.
Peace and her famous arts
Were yours: though tide on tide

Of Europe's battle scourged
Black field and reddened soil,
From blood and smoke emerged
Peace and her fruitful toil.

Yet when the challenge rang,
"The War-Lord comes; give room!"
Fearless to arms you sprang
Against the odds of doom.

Like your own Damien
Who sought that leper's isle
To die a simple man
For men with tranquil smile,

So strong in faith you dared
Defy the giant, scorn
Ignobly to be spared,
Though trampled, spoiled, and torn,

And in your faith arose
And smote, and smote again,

Till those astonished foes
Reeled from their mounds of slain,

The faith that the free soul,
Untaught by force to quail,
Through fire and dirge and dole
Prevails and shall prevail.

Still for your frontier stands
The host that knew no dread,
Your little, stubborn land's
Nameless, immortal dead.

Laurence Binyon

BELGIUM

La Belgique ne regrette rien

Not with her ruined silver spires,
Not with her cities shamed and rent,
Perish the imperishable fires
That shape the homestead from the tent.

Wherever men are staunch and free,
There shall she keep her fearless state,
And homeless, to great nations be
The home of all that makes them great.

Edith Wharton

TO BELGIUM

Champion of human honour, let us lave
    Your feet and bind your wounds on bended knee.
    Though coward hands have nailed you to the tree
And shed your innocent blood and dug your grave,

Rejoice and live! Your oriflamme shall wave—
While man has power to perish and be free—
A golden flame of holiest Liberty,
Proud as the dawn and as the sunset brave.

Belgium, where dwelleth reverence for right
Enthroned above all ideals; where your fate
And your supernal patience and your might
Most sacred grow in human estimate,
You shine a star above this stormy night
Little no more, but infinitely great.

Eden Phillpotts

TO BELGIUM IN EXILE

[Lines dedicated to one of her priests, by whose words they were prompted.]

Land of the desolate, Mother of tears,
Weeping your beauty marred and torn,
Your children tossed upon the spears,
Your altars rent, your hearths forlorn,
Where Spring has no renewing spell,
And Love no language save a long Farewell!

Ah, precious tears, and each a pearl,
Whose price—for so in God we trust
Who saw them fall in that blind swirl
Of ravening flame and reeking dust—
The spoiler with his life shall pay,
When Justice at the last demands her Day.

O tried and proved, whose record stands
Lettered in blood too deep to fade,
Take courage! Never in our hands
Shall the avenging sword be stayed

Till you are healed of all your pain,
And come with Honour to your own again.

Owen Seaman
May 19, 1915

THE WIFE OF FLANDERS

Low and brown barns, thatched and repatched and tattered,
Where I had seven sons until to-day,
A little hill of hay your spur has scattered . . .
This is not Paris. You have lost the way.

You, staring at your sword to find it brittle,
Surprised at the surprise that was your plan,
Who, shaking and breaking barriers not a little,
Find never more the death-door of Sedan—

Must I for more than carnage call you claimant,
Paying you a penny for each son you slay?
Man, the whole globe in gold were no repayment
For what *you* have lost. And how shall I repay?

What is the price of that red spark that caught me
From a kind farm that never had a name?
What is the price of that dead man they brought me?
For other dead men do not look the same.

How should I pay for one poor graven steeple
Whereon you shattered what you shall not know?
How should I pay you, miserable people?
How should I pay you everything you owe?

Unhappy, can I give you back your honour?
Though I forgave, would any man forget?
While all the great green land has trampled on her
The treason and terror of the night we met.

Not any more in vengeance or in pardon
An old wife bargains for a bean that's hers.
You have no word to break: no heart to harden.
Ride on and prosper. You have lost your spurs.

Gilbert Keith Chesterton

RUSSIA—AMERICA

A wind in the world! The dark departs;
The chains now rust that crushed men's flesh and bones,
Feet tread no more the mildewed prison stones,
And slavery is lifted from your hearts.

A wind in the world! O Company
Of darkened Russia, watching long in vain,
Now shall you see the cloud of Russia's pain
Go shrinking out across a summer sky.

A wind in the world! Our God shall be
In all the future left, no kingly doll
Decked out with dreadful sceptre, steel, and stole,
But walk the earth—a man, in Charity.

* * * * *

A wind in the world! And doubts are blown
To dust along, and the old stars come forth—
Stars of a creed to Pilgrim Fathers worth
A field of broken spears and flowers strown.

A wind in the world! Now truancy
From the true self is ended; to her part
Steadfast again she moves, and from her heart
A great America cries: Death to Tyranny!

A wind in the world! And we have come
Together, sea by sea; in all the lands

Vision doth move at last, and Freedom stands
With brightened wings, and smiles and beckons home!

John Galsworthy

TO RUSSIA NEW AND FREE

Land of the Martyrs—of the martyred dead
And martyred living—now of noble fame!
Long wert thou saddest of the nations, wed
To Sorrow as the fire to the flame,
Not yet relentless History had writ of Teuton shame.

Thou knewest all the gloom of hope deferred.
'Twixt God and Russia wrong had built such bar
Each by the other could no more be heard.
Seen through the cloud, the child's familiar star,
That once made Heaven near, had made it seem more far.

Land of the Breaking Dawn! No more look back
To that long night that nevermore can be:
The sunless dungeon and the exile's track.
To the world's dreams of terror let it flee.
To gentle April cruel March is now antiquity.

Yet—of the Past one sacred relic save:
That boundary-post 'twixt Russia and Despair,—
Set where the dead might look upon his grave,—
Kissed by him with his last-breathed Russian air.
Keep it to witness to the world what heroes still may dare.

Land of New Hope, no more the minor key,
No more the songs of exile long and lone;
Thy tears henceforth be tears of memory.
Sing, with the joy the joyless would have known
Who for this visioned happiness so gladly gave their own.

Land of the warm heart and the friendly hand,
Strike the free chord; no more the muted strings!

Forever let the equal record stand—
A thousand winters for this Spring of Springs,
That to a warring world, through thee, millennial longing brings.

On thy white tablets, cleansed of royal stain,
What message to the future mayst thou write!—
The People's Law, the bulwark of their reign,
And vigilant Liberty, of ancient might,
And Brotherhood, that can alone lead to the loftiest height.

Take, then, our hearts' rejoicing overflow,
Thou new-born daughter of Democracy,
Whose coming sets the expectant earth aglow.
Soon the glad skies thy proud new flag shall see,
And hear thy chanted hymns of hope for Russia new and free.

Robert Underwood Johnson
April, 1917

ITALY IN ARMS

Of all my dreams by night and day,
One dream will evermore return,
The dream of Italy in May;
The sky a brimming azure urn
Where lights of amber brood and burn;
The doves about San Marco's square,
The swimming Campanile tower,
The giants, hammering out the hour,
The palaces, the bright lagoons,
The gondolas gliding here and there
Upon the tide that sways and swoons.

The domes of San Antonio,
Where Padua 'mid her mulberry-trees
Reclines; Adige's crescent flow
Beneath Verona's balconies;

Rich Florence of the Medicis;
Sienna's starlike streets that climb
From hill to hill; Assisi well
Remembering the holy spell
Of rapt St. Francis; with her crown
Of battlements, embossed by time,
Stern old Perugia looking down.

Then, mother of great empires, Rome,
City of the majestic past,
That o'er far leagues of alien foam
The shadows of her eagles cast,
Imperious still; impending, vast,

The Colosseum's curving line;
Pillar and arch and colonnade;
St. Peter's consecrated shade,
And Hadrian's tomb where Tiber strays;
The ruins on the Palatine
With all their memories of dead days.

And Naples, with her sapphire arc
Of bay, her perfect sweep of shore;
Above her, like a demon stark,
The dark fire-mountain evermore
Looming portentous, as of yore;
Fair Capri with her cliffs and caves;
Salerno drowsing 'mid her vines
And olives, and the shattered shrines
Of Paestum where the gray ghosts tread,
And where the wilding rose still waves
As when by Greek girls garlanded.

But hark! What sound the ear dismays,
Mine Italy, mine Italy?
Thou that wert wrapt in peace, the haze
Of loveliness spread over thee!
Yet since the grapple needs must be,
I who have wandered in the night

With Dante, Petrarch's Laura known,
Seen Vallombrosa's groves breeze-blown,
Met Angelo and Raffael,
Against iconoclastic might
In this grim hour must wish thee well!

Clinton Scollard

ON THE ITALIAN FRONT, MCMXVI

"I will die cheering, if I needs must die;
So shall my last breath write upon my lips
Viva Italia! when my spirit slips
Down the great darkness from the mountain sky;
And those who shall behold me where I lie
Shall murmur: 'Look, you! how his spirit dips
From glory into glory! the eclipse
Of death is vanquished! Lo, his victor-cry!'

"Live, thou, upon my lips, Italia mine,
The sacred death-cry of my frozen clay!
Let thy dear light from my dead body shine
And to the passer-by thy message say:
'Ecco! though heaven has made my skies divine,
My sons' love sanctifies my soil for aye!'"

George Edward Woodberry

AUSTRALIA TO ENGLAND

By all the deeds to Thy dear glory done,
By all the life blood, spilt to serve Thy need,
By all the fettered lives Thy touch hath freed,
By all Thy dream in us anew begun;
By all the guerdon English sire to son
Hath given of highest vision, kingliest deed,
By all Thine agony, of God decreed
For trial and strength, our fate with Thine is one.

Still dwells Thy spirit in our hearts and lips,
Honour and life we hold from none but Thee,
And if we live Thy pensioners no more
But seek a nation's might of men and ships,
'T is but that when the world is black with war
Thy sons may stand beside Thee strong and free.

Archibald T. Strong
August, 1914

CANADA TO ENGLAND

Great names of thy great captains gone before
Beat with our blood, who have that blood of thee:
Raleigh and Grenville, Wolfe, and all the free
Fine souls who dared to front a world in war.
Such only may outreach the envious years
Where feebler crowns and fainter stars remove,
Nurtured in one remembrance and one love
Too high for passion and too stern for tears.

O little isle our fathers held for home,
Not, not alone thy standards and thy hosts
Lead where thy sons shall follow, Mother Land:
Quick as the north wind, ardent as the foam,
Behold, behold the invulnerable ghosts
Of all past greatnesses about thee stand.

Marjorie L.C. Pickthall

LANGEMARCK AT YPRES

This is the ballad of Langemarck,
A story of glory and might;
Of the vast Hun horde, and Canada's part
In the great grim fight.

It was April fair on the Flanders Fields,
But the dreadest April then

That ever the years, in their fateful flight,
Had brought to this world of men.

North and east, a monster wall,
The mighty Hun ranks lay,
With fort on fort, and iron-ringed trench,
Menacing, grim and gray.

And south and west, like a serpent of fire,
Serried the British lines,
And in between, the dying and dead,
And the stench of blood, and the trampled mud,
On the fair, sweet Belgian vines.

And far to the eastward, harnessed and taut,
Like a scimitar, shining and keen,
Gleaming out of that ominous gloom,
Old France's hosts were seen.

When out of the grim Hun lines one night,
There rolled a sinister smoke;—
A strange, weird cloud, like a pale, green shroud,
And death lurked in its cloak.

On a fiend-like wind it curled along
Over the brave French ranks,
Like a monster tree its vapours spread,
In hideous, burning banks
Of poisonous fumes that scorched the night
With their sulphurous demon danks.

And men went mad with horror, and fled
From that terrible, strangling death,
That seemed to sear both body and soul
With its baleful, flaming breath.

Till even the little dark men of the south,
Who feared neither God nor man,

Those fierce, wild fighters of Afric's steppes,
Broke their battalions and ran:—

Ran as they never had run before,
Gasping, and fainting for breath;
For they knew 't was no human foe that slew;
And that hideous smoke meant death.

Then red in the reek of that evil cloud,
The Hun swept over the plain;
And the murderer's dirk did its monster work,
'Mid the scythe-like shrapnel rain;

Till it seemed that at last the brute Hun hordes
Had broken that wall of steel;
And that soon, through this breach in the freeman's dyke,
His trampling hosts would wheel;—

And sweep to the south in ravaging might,
And Europe's peoples again
Be trodden under the tyrant's heel,
Like herds, in the Prussian pen.

But in that line on the British right,
There massed a corps amain,
Of men who hailed from a far west land
Of mountain and forest and plain;

Men new to war and its dreadest deeds,
But noble and staunch and true;
Men of the open, East and West,
Brew of old Britain's brew.

These were the men out there that night,
When Hell loomed close ahead;
Who saw that pitiful, hideous rout,
And breathed those gases dread;
While some went under and some went mad;
But never a man there fled.

For the word was "Canada," theirs to fight,
  And keep on fighting still;—
Britain said, fight, and fight they would,
Though the Devil himself in sulphurous mood
  Came over that hideous hill.

Yea, stubborn, they stood, that hero band,
  Where no soul hoped to live;
For five, 'gainst eighty thousand men,
  Were hopeless odds to give.

Yea, fought they on! 'T was Friday eve,
  When that demon gas drove down;
'T was Saturday eve that saw them still
  Grimly holding their own;

Sunday, Monday, saw them yet,
  A steadily lessening band,
With "no surrender" in their hearts,
  But the dream of a far-off land,

Where mother and sister and love would weep
  For the hushed heart lying still;—
But never a thought but to do their part,
  And work the Empire's will.

Ringed round, hemmed in, and back to back,
  They fought there under the dark,
And won for Empire, God and Right,
  At grim, red Langemarck.

Wonderful battles have shaken this world,
  Since the Dawn-God overthrew Dis;
Wonderful struggles of right against wrong,
Sung in the rhymes of the world's great song,
  But never a greater than this.

Bannockburn, Inkerman, Balaclava,
  Marathon's godlike stand;

But never a more heroic deed,
And never a greater warrior breed,
  In any war-man's land.

This is the ballad of Langemarck,
  A story of glory and might;
Of the vast Hun horde, and Canada's part
  In the great, grim fight.

Wilfred Campbell

CANADIANS

With arrows on their quarters and with numbers on their hoofs,
With the trampling sound of twenty that re-echoes in the roofs,
Low of crest and dull of coat, wan and wild of eye,
Through our English village the Canadians go by.

Shying at a passing cart, swerving from a car,
Tossing up an anxious head to flaunt a snowy star,
Racking at a Yankee gait, reaching at the rein,
Twenty raw Canadians are tasting life again!

Hollow-necked and hollow-flanked, lean of rib and hip,
Strained and sick and weary with the wallow of the ship,
Glad to smell the turf again, hear the robin's call,
Tread again the country road they lost at Montreal!

Fate may bring them dule and woe; better steeds than they
Sleep beside the English guns a hundred leagues away;
But till war hath need of them, lightly lie their reins,
Softly fall the feet of them along the English lanes.

Will H. Ogilvie

THE KAISER AND BELGIUM

He said: "Thou petty people, let me pass.
  What canst thou do but bow to me and kneel?"
But sudden a dry land caught fire like grass,
  And answer hurtled but from shell and steel.

He looked for silence, but a thunder came
  Upon him, from Liège a leaden hail.
All Belgium flew up at his throat in flame
  Till at her gates amazed his legions quail.

Take heed, for now on haunted ground they tread;
  There bowed a mightier war lord to his fall:
Fear! lest that very green grass again grow red
  With blood of German now as then with Gaul.

If him whom God destroys He maddens first,
Then thy destruction slake thy madman's thirst.

Stephen Phillips

THE BATTLE OF LIÈGE

Now spake the Emperor to all his shining battle forces,
To the Lancers, and the Rifles, to the Gunners and the
  Horses;—
And his pride surged up within him as he saw their banners
  stream!—
"'T is a twelve-day march to Paris, by the road our fathers
  travelled,
And the prize is half an empire when the scarlet road's
  unravelled—
Go you now across the border,
God's decree and William's order—
Climb the frowning Belgian ridges
With your naked swords agleam!
Seize the City of the Bridges—
Then get on, get on to Paris—

To the jewelled streets of Paris—
To the lovely woman, Paris, that has driven me to dream!"

A hundred thousand fighting men
They climbed the frowning ridges,
With their flaming swords drawn free
And their pennants at their knee.
They went up to their desire,
To the City of the Bridges,
With their naked brands outdrawn
Like the lances of the dawn!
In a swelling surf of fire,
Crawling higher—higher—higher—
Till they crumpled up and died
Like a sudden wasted tide,
And the thunder in their faces beat them down and flung
them wide!

They had paid a thousand men,
Yet they formed and came again,
For they heard the silver bugles sounding challenge to their
pride,
And they rode with swords agleam
For the glory of a dream,
And they stormed up to the cannon's mouth and withered
there, and died . . .
The daylight lay in ashes
On the blackened western hill,
And the dead were calm and still;
But the Night was torn with gashes—
Sudden ragged crimson gashes—
And the siege-guns snarled and roared,
With their flames thrust like a sword,
And the tranquil moon came riding on the heaven's silver
ford.

What a fearful world was there,
Tangled in the cold moon's hair!
Man and beast lay hurt and screaming,

(Men must die when Kings are dreaming!)—
While within the harried town
Mothers dragged their children down
As the awful rain came screaming,
For the glory of a Crown!

So the Morning flung her cloak
Through the hanging pall of smoke—
Trimmed with red, it was, and dripping with a deep and angry stain!
And the Day came walking then
Through a lane of murdered men,
And her light fell down before her like a Cross upon the plain!
But the forts still crowned the height
With a bitter iron crown!
They had lived to flame and fight,
They had lived to keep the Town!
And they poured their havoc down
All that day . . . and all that night . . .
While four times their number came,
Pawns that played a bloody game!—
With a silver trumpeting,
For the glory of the King,
To the barriers of the thunder and the fury of the flame!

So they stormed the iron Hill,
O'er the sleepers lying still,
And their trumpets sang them forward through the dull succeeding dawns,
But the thunder flung them wide,
And they crumpled up and died,—
They had waged the war of monarchs—and they died the death of pawns.

But the forts still stood . . . Their breath
Swept the foeman like a blade,
Though ten thousand men were paid
To the hungry purse of Death,

Though the field was wet with blood,
Still the bold defences stood,
Stood!

And the King came out with his bodyguard at the day's departing gleam—
And the moon rode up behind the smoke and showed the King his dream.

Dana Burnet

MEN OF VERDUN

There are five men in the moonlight
That by their shadows stand;
Three hobble humped on crutches,
And two lack each a hand.

Frogs somewhere near the roadside
Chorus their chant absorbed:
But a hush breathes out of the dream-light
That far in heaven is orbed.

It is gentle as sleep falling
And wide as thought can span,
The ancient peace and wonder
That brims the heart of man.

Beyond the hills it shines now
On no peace but the dead,
On reek of trenches thunder-shocked,
Tense fury of wills in wrestle locked,
A chaos crumbled red!

The five men in the moonlight
Chat, joke, or gaze apart.
They talk of days and comrades,
But each one hides his heart.

They wear clean cap and tunic,
As when they went to war;
A gleam comes where the medal's pinned:
But they will fight no more.

The shadows, maimed and antic,
Gesture and shape distort,
Like mockery of a demon dumb
Out of the hell-din whence they come
That dogs them for his sport:

But as if dead men were risen
And stood before me there
With a terrible fame about them blown
In beams of spectral air,

I see them, men transfigured
As in a dream, dilate
Fabulous with the Titan-throb
Of battling Europe's fate;

For history's hushed before them,
And legend flames afresh,—
Verdun, the name of thunder,
Is written on their flesh.

Laurence Binyon

VERDUN

Three hundred thousand men, but not enough
To break this township on a winding stream;
More yet must fall, and more, ere the red stuff
That built a nation's manhood may redeem
The Master's hopes and realize his dream.

They pave the way to Verdun; on their dust
The Hohenzollerns mount and, hand in hand,
Gaze haggard south; for yet another thrust

And higher hills must heap, ere they may stand
To feed their eyes upon the promised land.

One barrow, borne of women, lifts them high,
Built up of many a thousand human dead.
Nursed on their mothers' bosoms, now they lie—
A Golgotha, all shattered, torn and sped,
A mountain for these royal feet to tread.

A Golgotha, upon whose carrion clay
Justice of myriad men still in the womb
Shall heave two crosses; crucify and flay
Two memories accurs'd; then in the tomb
Of world-wide execration give them room.

Verdun! A clarion thy name shall ring
Adown the ages and the Nations see
Thy monuments of glory. Now we bring
Thank-offering and bend the reverent knee,
Thou star upon the crown of Liberty!

Eden Phillpotts

GUNS OF VERDUN

Guns of Verdun point to Metz
From the plated parapets;
Guns of Metz grin back again
O'er the fields of fair Lorraine.

Guns of Metz are long and grey,
Growling through a summer day;
Guns of Verdun, grey and long,
Boom an echo of their song.

Guns of Metz to Verdun roar,
"Sisters, you shall foot the score;"
Guns of Verdun say to Metz,
"Fear not, for we pay our debts."

Guns of Metz they grumble, "When?"
Guns of Verdun answer then,
"Sisters, when to guard Lorraine
Gunners lay you East again!"

Patrick R. Chalmers

THE SPIRES OF OXFORD

I saw the spires of Oxford
  As I was passing by,
The gray spires of Oxford
  Against the pearl-gray sky.
My heart was with the Oxford men
  Who went abroad to die.

The years go fast in Oxford,
  The golden years and gay,
The hoary Colleges look down
  On careless boys at play.
But when the bugles sounded war
  They put their games away.

They left the peaceful river,
  The cricket-field, the quad,
The shaven lawns of Oxford,
  To seek a bloody sod—
They gave their merry youth away
  For country and for God.

God rest you, happy gentlemen,
  Who laid your good lives down,
Who took the khaki and the gun
  Instead of cap and gown.
God bring you to a fairer place
  Than even Oxford town.

Winifred M. Letts

OXFORD IN WAR-TIME

[The Boat Race will not be held this year (1915). The whole of last year's Oxford Eight and the great majority of the cricket and football teams are serving the King.]

Under the tow-path past the barges
  Never an eight goes flashing by;
Never a blatant coach on the marge is
  Urging his crew to do or die;
Never the critic we knew enlarges,
  Fluent, on How and Why!

Once by the Iffley Road November
  Welcomed the Football men aglow,
Covered with mud, as you'll remember,
  Eager to vanquish Oxford's foe.
Where are the teams of last December?
  Gone—where they had to go!

Where are her sons who waged at cricket
  Warfare against the foeman-friend?
Far from the Parks, on a harder wicket,
  Still they attack and still defend;
Playing a greater game, they'll stick it,
  Fearless until the end!

Oxford's goodliest children leave her,
  Hastily thrusting books aside;
Still the hurrying weeks bereave her,
  Filling her heart with joy and pride;
Only the thought of you can grieve her,
  You who have fought and died.

W. Snow

OXFORD REVISITED IN WAR-TIME

Beneath fair Magdalen's storied towers
I wander in a dream,
And hear the mellow chimes float out
O'er Cherwell's ice-bound stream.

Throstle and blackbird stiff with cold
Hop on the frozen grass;
Among the aged, upright oaks
The dun deer slowly pass.

The chapel organ rolls and swells,
And voices still praise God;
But ah! the thought of youthful friends
Who lie beneath the sod.

Now wounded men with gallant eyes
Go hobbling down the street,
And nurses from the hospitals
Speed by with tireless feet.

The town is full of uniforms,
And through the stormy sky,
Frightening the rooks from the tallest trees,
The aeroplanes roar by.

The older faces still are here,
More grave and true and kind,
Ennobled by the steadfast toil
Of patient heart and mind.

And old-time friends are dearer grown
To fill a double place:
Unshaken faith makes glorious
Each forward-looking face.

Old Oxford walls are grey and worn:
She knows the truth of tears,

But to-day she stands in her ancient pride
Crowned with eternal years.

Gone are her sons: yet her heart is glad
In the glory of their youth,
For she brought them forth to live or die
By freedom, justice, truth.

Cold moonlight falls on silent towers;
The young ghosts walk with the old;
But Oxford dreams of the dawn of May
And her heart is free and bold.

Tertius van Dyke
Magdalen College,
January, 1917

SONNETS WRITTEN IN THE FALL OF 1914

I

Awake, ye nations, slumbering supine,
  Who round enring the European fray!
  Heard ye the trumpet sound? "The Day! the Day!
The last that shall on England's Empire shine!
The Parliament that broke the Right Divine
  Shall see her realm of reason swept away,
  And lesser nations shall the sword obey—
The sword o'er all carve the great world's design!"

So on the English Channel boasts the foe
  On whose imperial brow death's helmet nods.
Look where his hosts o'er bloody Belgium go,
  And mix a nation's past with blazing sods!
A kingdom's waste! a people's homeless woe!
  Man's broken Word, and violated gods!

II

Far fall the day when England's realm shall see
The sunset of dominion! Her increase
Abolishes the man-dividing seas,
And frames the brotherhood on earth to be!
She, in free peoples planting sovereignty,
Orbs half the civil world in British peace;
And though time dispossess her, and she cease,
Rome-like she greatens in man's memory.

Oh, many a crown shall sink in war's turmoil,
And many a new republic light the sky,
Fleets sweep the ocean, nations till the soil,
Genius be born and generations die.
Orient and Occident together toil,
Ere such a mighty work man rears on high!

III

Hearken, the feet of the Destroyer tread
The wine-press of the nations; fast the blood
Pours from the side of Europe; in the flood
On the septentrional watershed
The rivers of fair France are running red!
England, the mother-aerie of our brood,
That on the summit of dominion stood,
Shakes in the blast: heaven battles overhead!

Lift up thy head, O Rheims, of ages heir
That treasured up in thee their glorious sum;
Upon whose brow, prophetically fair,
Flamed the great morrow of the world to come;
Haunt with thy beauty this volcanic air
Ere yet thou close, O Flower of Christendom!

IV

As when the shadow of the sun's eclipse
    Sweeps on the earth, and spreads a spectral air,
    As if the universe were dying there,
On continent and isle the darkness dips
Unwonted gloom, and on the Atlantic slips;
    So in the night the Belgian cities flare
    Horizon-wide; the wandering people fare
Along the roads, and load the fleeing ships.

And westward borne that planetary sweep
    Darkening o'er England and her times to be,
Already steps upon the ocean-deep!
    Watch well, my country, that unearthly sea,
Lest when thou thinkest not, and in thy sleep,
    Unapt for war, that gloom enshadow thee.

V

I pray for peace; yet peace is but a prayer.
    How many wars have been in my brief years!
    All races and all faiths, both hemispheres,
My eyes have seen embattled everywhere
The wide earth through; yet do I not despair
    Of peace, that slowly through far ages nears;
    Though not to me the golden morn appears,
My faith is perfect in time's issue fair.

For man doth build on an eternal scale,
    And his ideals are framed of hope deferred;
The millennium came not; yet Christ did not fail,
    Though ever unaccomplished is His word;
Him Prince of Peace, though unenthroned, we hail,
    Supreme when in all bosoms He be heard.

VI

This is my faith, and my mind's heritage,
Wherein I toil, though in a lonely place,
Who yet world-wide survey the human race
Unequal from wild nature disengage
Body and soul, and life's old strife assuage;
Still must abide, till heaven perfect its grace,
And love grown wisdom sweeten in man's face,
Alike the Christian and the heathen rage.

The tutelary genius of mankind
Ripens by slow degrees the final State,
That in the soul shall its foundations find
And only in victorious love grow great;
Patient the heart must be, humble the mind,
That doth the greater births of time await!

VII

Whence not unmoved I see the nations form
From Dover to the fountains of the Rhine,
A hundred leagues, the scarlet battle-line,
And by the Vistula great armies swarm,
A vaster flood; rather my breast grows warm,
Seeing all peoples of the earth combine
Under one standard, with one countersign,
Grown brothers in the universal storm.

And never through the wide world yet there rang
A mightier summons! O Thou who from the side
Of Athens and the loins of Casar sprang,
Strike, Europe, with half the coming world allied
For those ideals for which, since Homer sang,
The hosts of thirty centuries have died.

George Edward Woodberry

THE WAR FILMS

O living pictures of the dead,
  O songs without a sound,
O fellowship whose phantom tread
  Hallows a phantom ground—
How in a gleam have these revealed
  The faith we had not found.

We have sought God in a cloudy Heaven,
  We have passed by God on earth:
His seven sins and his sorrows seven,
  His wayworn mood and mirth,
Like a ragged cloak have hid from us
  The secret of his birth.

Brother of men, when now I see
  The lads go forth in line,
Thou knowest my heart is hungry in me
  As for thy bread and wine;
Thou knowest my heart is bowed in me
  To take their death for mine.

Henry Newbolt

THE SEARCHLIGHTS

[Political morality differs from individual morality, because there is no power above the State.—*General von Bernhardi*]

Shadow by shadow, stripped for fight,
  The lean black cruisers search the sea.
Night-long their level shafts of light
  Revolve, and find no enemy.
Only they know each leaping wave
May hide the lightning, and their grave.

And in the land they guard so well
  Is there no silent watch to keep?

An age is dying, and the bell
  Rings midnight on a vaster deep.
But over all its waves, once more
The searchlights move, from shore to shore.

And captains that we thought were dead,
  And dreamers that we thought were dumb,
And voices that we thought were fled,
  Arise, and call us, and we come;
And "Search in thine own soul," they cry;
"For there, too, lurks thine enemy."

Search for the foe in thine own soul,
  The sloth, the intellectual pride;
The trivial jest that veils the goal
  For which, our fathers lived and died;
The lawless dreams, the cynic Art,
That rend thy nobler self apart.

Not far, not far into the night,
  These level swords of light can pierce;
Yet for her faith does England fight,
  Her faith in this our universe,
Believing Truth and Justice draw
From founts of everlasting law;

The law that rules the stars, our stay,
  Our compass through the world's wide sea.
The one sure light, the one sure way,
  The one firm base of Liberty;
The one firm road that men have trod
Through Chaos to the throne of God.

Therefore a Power above the State,
  The unconquerable Power, returns,
The fire, the fire that made her great
  Once more upon her altar burns,

Once more, redeemed and healed and whole,
She moves to the Eternal Goal.

Alfred Noyes

CHRISTMAS: 1915

Now is the midnight of the nations: dark
  Even as death, beside her blood-dark seas,
  Earth, like a mother in birth agonies,
Screams in her travail, and the planets hark
Her million-throated terror. Naked, stark,
  Her torso writhes enormous, and her knees
  Shudder against the shadowed Pleiades,
Wrenching the night's imponderable arc.

Christ! What shall be delivered to the morn
  Out of these pangs, if ever indeed another
  Morn shall succeed this night, or this vast mother
Survive to know the blood-spent offspring, torn
  From her racked flesh?—What splendour from the smother?
What new-wing'd world, or mangled god still-born?

Percy MacKaye

"MEN WHO MARCH AWAY"

(SONG OF THE SOLDIERS)

What of the faith and fire within us
  Men who march away
  Ere the barn-cocks say
  Night is growing gray,
To hazards whence no tears can win us;
What of the faith and fire within us
  Men who march away!

Is it a purblind prank, O think you,
    Friend with the musing eye
    Who watch us stepping by,
    With doubt and dolorous sigh?
Can much pondering so hoodwink you?
Is it a purblind prank, O think you,
    Friend with the musing eye?

Nay. We see well what we are doing,
    Though some may not see—
    Dalliers as they be—
    England's need are we;
Her distress would leave us rueing;
Nay. We well see what we are doing,
    Though some may not see!

In our heart of hearts believing
    Victory crowns the just,
    And that braggarts must
    Surely bite the dust,
Press we to the field ungrieving,
In our heart of hearts believing
    Victory crowns the just.

Hence the faith and fire within us
    Men who march away
    Ere the barn-cocks say
    Night is growing gray,
To hazards whence no tears can win us;
Hence the faith and fire within us
    Men who march away.

Thomas Hardy
September 5, 1914

WE WILLED IT NOT

We willed it not. We have not lived in hate,
Loving too well the shires of England thrown
From sea to sea to covet your estate,
Or wish one flight of fortune from your throne.

We had grown proud because the nations stood
Hoping together against the calumny
That, tortured of its old barbarian blood,
Barbarian still the heart of man should be.

Builders there are who name you overlord,
Building with us the citadels of light,
Who hold as we this chartered sin abhorred,
And cry you risen Caesar of the Night.

Beethoven speaks with Milton on this day,
And Shakespeare's word with Goethe's beats the sky,
In witness of the birthright you betray,
In witness of the vision you deny.

We love the hearth, the quiet hills, the song,
The friendly gossip come from every land;
And very peace were now a nameless wrong—
You thrust this bitter quarrel to our hand.

For this your pride the tragic armies go,
And the grim navies watch along the seas;
You trade in death, you mock at life, you throw
To God the tumult of your blasphemies.

You rob us of our love-right. It is said.
In treason to the world, you are enthroned,
We rise, and, by the yet ungathered dead,
Not lightly shall the treason be atoned.

John Drinkwater

THE DEATH OF PEACE

Now slowly sinks the day-long labouring Sun
Behind the tranquil trees and old church-tower;
And we who watch him know our day is done;
For us too comes the evening—and the hour.

The sunbeams slanting through those ancient trees,
The sunlit lichens burning on the byre,
The lark descending, and the homing bees,
Proclaim the sweet relief all things desire.

Golden the river brims beneath the west,
And holy peace to all the world is given;
The songless stockdove preens her ruddied breast;
The blue smoke windeth like a prayer to heaven.

* * * * *

O old, old England, land of golden peace,
Thy fields are spun with gossameres of gold,
And golden garners gather thy increase,
And plenty crowns thy loveliness untold.

By sunlight or by starlight ever thou
Art excellent in beauty manifold;
The still star victory ever gems thy brow;
Age cannot age thee, ages make thee old.

Thy beauty brightens with the evening sun
Across the long-lit meads and distant spire:
So sleep thou well—like his thy labour done;
Rest in thy glory as he rests in fire.

* * * * *

But even in this hour of soft repose
A gentle sadness chides us like a friend—
The sorrow of the joy that overflows,
The burden of the beauty that must end.

And from the fading sunset comes a cry,
And in the twilight voices wailing past,
Like wild-swans calling, "When we rest we die,
And woe to them that linger and are last";

And as the Sun sinks, sudden in heav'n new born
There shines an armed Angel like a Star,
Who cries above the darkling world in scorn,
"God comes to Judgment. Learn ye what ye are."

* * * * *

From fire to umber fades the sunset-gold,
From umber into silver and twilight;
The infant flowers their orisons have told
And turn together folded for the night;

The garden urns are black against the eve;
The white moth flitters through the fragrant glooms;
How beautiful the heav'ns!—But yet we grieve
And wander restless from the lighted rooms.

For through the world to-night a murmur thrills
As at some new-born prodigy of time—
Peace dies like twilight bleeding on the hills,
And Darkness creeps to hide the hateful crime.

Art thou no more, O Maiden Heaven-born
O Peace, bright Angel of the windless morn?
Who comest down to bless our furrow'd fields,
Or stand like Beauty smiling 'mid the corn:

Mistress of mirth and ease and summer dreams,
Who lingerest among the woods and streams
To help us heap the harvest 'neath the moon,
And homeward laughing lead the lumb'ring teams:

Who teachest to our children thy wise lore;
Who keepest full the goodman's golden store;

Who crownest Life with plenty, Death with flow'rs;
Peace, Queen of Kindness—but of earth, no more.

* * * * *

Not thine but ours the fault, thy care was vain;
For this that we have done be ours the pain;
Thou gayest much, as He who gave us all,
And as we slew Him for it thou art slain.

Heav'n left to men the moulding of their fate:
To live as wolves or pile the pillar'd State—
Like boars and bears to grunt and growl in mire,
Or dwell aloft, effulgent gods, elate.

Thou liftedst us: we slew and with thee fell—
From golden thrones of wisdom weeping fell.
Fate rends the chaplets from our feeble brows;
The spires of Heaven fade in fogs of hell.

* * * * *

She faints, she falls; her dying eyes are dim;
Her fingers play with those bright buds she bore
To please us, but that she can bring no more;
And dying yet she smiles—as Christ on him
Who slew Him slain. Her eyes so beauteous
Are lit with tears shed—not for herself but us.

The gentle Beings of the hearth and home;
The lovely Dryads of her aisled woods;
The Angels that do dwell in solitudes
Where she dwelleth; and joyous Spirits that roam
To bless her bleating flocks and fruitful lands;
Are gather'd there to weep, and kiss her dying hands.

"Look, look," they cry, "she is not dead, she breathes!
And we have staunched the damned wound and deep,
The cavern-carven wound. She doth but sleep
And will awake. Bring wine, and new-wound wreaths

Wherewith to crown awaking her dear head,
And make her Queen again."—But no, for Peace was dead.

* * * * *

And then there came black Lords; and Dwarfs obscene
With lavish tongues; and Trolls; and treacherous Things
Like loose-lipp'd Councillors and cruel Kings
Who sharpen lies and daggers subterrene:
And flashed their evil eyes and weeping cried,
"We ruled the world for Peace. By her own hand she died."

* * * * *

In secret he made sharp the bitter blade,
And poison'd it with bane of lies and drew,
And stabb'd—O God! the Cruel Cripple slew;
And cowards fled or lent him trembling aid,
She fell and died—in all the tale of time
The direst deed e'er done, the most accursed crime.

Ronald Ross

IN WAR-TIME

(AN AMERICAN HOMEWARD-BOUND)

Further and further we leave the scene
  Of war—and of England's care;
I try to keep my mind serene—
  But my heart stays there;

For a distant song of pain and wrong
  My spirit doth deep confuse,
And I sit all day on the deck, and long—
  And long for news!

I seem to see them in battle-line—
  Heroes with hearts of gold,

But of their victory a sign
  The Fates withhold;

And the hours too tardy-footed pass,
  The voiceless hush grows dense
'Mid the imaginings, alas!
  That feed suspense.

Oh, might I lie on the wind, or fly
  In the wilful sea-bird's track,
Would I hurry on, with a homesick cry—
  Or hasten back?

Florence Earle Coates

THE ANVIL

Burned from the ore's rejected dross,
The iron whitens in the heat.
With plangent strokes of pain and loss
The hammers on the iron beat.
Searched by the fire, through death and dole
We feel the iron in our soul.

O dreadful Forge! if torn and bruised
The heart, more urgent comes our cry
Not to be spared but to be used,
Brain, sinew, and spirit, before we die.
Beat out the iron, edge it keen,
And shape us to the end we mean!

Laurence Binyon

THE FOOL RINGS HIS BELLS

Come, Death, I'd have a word with thee;
And thou, poor Innocency;
And Love—a lad with broken wing;
And Pity, too:

The Fool shall sing to you,
As Fools will sing.

Ay, music hath small sense,
And a tune's soon told,
And Earth is old,
And my poor wits are dense;
Yet have I secrets,—dark, my dear,
To breathe you all: Come near.
And lest some hideous listener tells,
I'll ring my bells.

They're all at war!
Yes, yes, their bodies go
'Neath burning sun and icy star
To chaunted songs of woe,
Dragging cold cannon through a mud
Of rain and blood;
The new moon glinting hard on eyes
Wide with insanities!

Hush! . . . I use words
I hardly know the meaning of;
And the mute birds
Are glancing at Love!
From out their shade of leaf and flower,
Trembling at treacheries

Which even in noonday cower,
Heed, heed not what I said
Of frenzied hosts of men,
More fools than I,
On envy, hatred fed,
Who kill, and die—
Spake I not plainly, then?
Yet Pity whispered, "Why?"

Thou silly thing, off to thy daisies go.
Mine was not news for child to know,

And Death—no ears hath. He hath supped where creep
Eyeless worms in hush of sleep;
Yet, when he smiles, the hand he draws
Athwart his grinning jaws
Faintly their thin bones rattle, and . . . There, there;
Hearken how my bells in the air
Drive away care! . . .

Nay, but a dream I had
Of a world all mad.
Not a simple happy mad like me,
Who am mad like an empty scene
Of water and willow tree,
Where the wind hath been;
But that foul Satan-mad,
Who rots in his own head,
And counts the dead,
Not honest one—and two—
But for the ghosts they were,
Brave, faithful, true,
When, head in air,
In Earth's dear green and blue
Heaven they did share
With Beauty who bade them there . . .

There, now! he goes—
Old Bones; I've wearied him.
Ay, and the light doth dim,
And asleep's the rose,
And tired Innocence
In dreams is hence . . .
Come, Love, my lad,
Nodding that drowsy head,
'T is time thy prayers were said.

Walter de la Mare

THE ROAD TO DIEPPE

[Concerning the experiences of a journey on foot through the night of August 4, 1914 (the night after the formal declaration of war between England and Germany), from a town near Amiens, in France, to Dieppe, a distance of somewhat more than forty miles.]

Before I knew, the Dawn was on the road,
Close at my side, so silently he came
Nor gave a sign of salutation, save
To touch with light my sleeve and make the way
Appear as if a shining countenance
Had looked on it. Strange was this radiant Youth,
As I, to these fair, fertile parts of France,
Where Caesar with his legions once had passed,
And where the Kaiser's Uhlans yet would pass
Or e'er another moon should cope with clouds
For mastery of these same fields.—To-night
(And but a month has gone since I walked there)
Well might the Kaiser write, as Caesar wrote,
In his new Commentaries on a Gallic war,
"*Fortissimi Belgae.*"—A moon ago!
Who would have then divined that dead would lie
Like swaths of grain beneath the harvest moon
Upon these lands the ancient Belgae held,
From Normandy beyond renowned Liège!—

But it was out of that dread August night
From which all Europe woke to war, that we,
This beautiful Dawn-Youth, and I, had come,
He from afar. Beyond grim Petrograd
He'd waked the moujik from his peaceful dreams,
Bid the muezzin call to morning prayer
Where minarets rise o'er the Golden Horn,
And driven shadows from the Prussian march
To lie beneath the lindens of the *stadt.*
Softly he'd stirred the bells to ring at Rheims,
He'd knocked at high Montmartre, hardly asleep;

Heard the sweet carillon of doomed Louvain,
Boylike, had tarried for a moment's play
Amid the traceries of Amiens,
And then was hast'ning on the road to Dieppe,
When he o'ertook me drowsy from the hours
Through which I'd walked, with no companions else
Than ghostly kilometer posts that stood
As sentinels' of space along the way.—
Often, in doubt, I'd paused to question one,
With nervous hands, as they who read Moon-type;
And more than once I'd caught a moment's sleep
Beside the highway, in the dripping grass,
While one of these white sentinels stood guard,
Knowing me for a friend, who loves the road,
And best of all by night, when wheels do sleep
And stars alone do walk abroad.—But once
Three watchful shadows, deeper than the dark,
Laid hands on me and searched me for the marks
Of traitor or of spy, only to find
Over my heart the badge of loyalty.—
With wish for *bon voyage* they gave me o'er
To the white guards who led me on again.

Thus Dawn o'ertook me and with magic speech
Made me forget the night as we strode on.
Where'er he looked a miracle was wrought:
A tree grew from the darkness at a glance;
A hut was thatched; a new chateau was reared
Of stone, as weathered as the church at Caen;
Gray blooms were coloured suddenly in red;
A flag was flung across the eastern sky.—
Nearer at hand, he made me then aware
Of peasant women bending in the fields,
Cradling and gleaning by the first scant light,
Their sons and husbands somewhere o'er the edge
Of these green-golden fields which they had sowed,
But will not reap,—out somewhere on the march,
God but knows where and if they come again.
One fallow field he pointed out to me

Where but the day before a peasant ploughed,
Dreaming of next year's fruit, and there his plough
Stood now mid-field, his horses commandeered,
A monstrous sable crow perched on the beam.

Before I knew, the Dawn was on the road,
Far from my side, so silently he went,
Catching his golden helmet as he ran,
And hast'ning on along the dun straight way,
Where old men's sabots now began to clack
And withered women, knitting, led their cows,
On, on to call the men of Kitchener
Down to their coasts,—I shouting after him:
"O Dawn, would you had let the world sleep on
Till all its armament were turned to rust,
Nor waked it to this day of hideous hate,
Of man's red murder and of woman's woe!"

Famished and lame, I came at last to Dieppe,
But Dawn had made his way across the sea,
And, as I climbed with heavy feet the cliff,
Was even then upon the sky-built towers
Of that great capital where nations all,
Teuton, Italian, Gallic, English, Slav,
Forget long hates in one consummate faith.

John Finley

TO FELLOW TRAVELLERS IN GREECE

MARCH-SEPTEMBER, 1914

'T was in the piping tune of peace
We trod the sacred soil of Greece,
Nor thought, where the Ilissus runs,
Of Teuton craft or Teuton guns;

Nor dreamt that, ere the year was spent,
Their iron challenge insolent

Would round the world's horizons pour,
From Europe to the Australian shore.

The tides of war had ebb'd away
From Trachis and Thermopylae,
Long centuries had come and gone
Since that fierce day at Marathon;

Freedom was firmly based, and we
Wall'd by our own encircling sea;
The ancient passions dead, and men
Battl'd with ledger and with pen.

So seem'd it, but to them alone
The wisdom of the gods is known;
Lest freedom's price decline, from far
Zeus hurl'd the thunderbolt of war.

And so once more the Persian steel
The armies of the Greeks must feel,
And once again a Xerxes know
The virtue of a Spartan foe.

Thus may the cloudy fates unroll'd
Retrace the starry circles old,
And the recurrent heavens decree
A Periclean dynasty.

W. Macneile Dixon

"WHEN THERE IS PEACE"

"When there is Peace our land no more
Will be the land we knew of yore."
Thus do our facile seers foretell
The truth that none can buy or sell
And e'en the wisest must ignore.

When we have bled at every pore,
Shall we still strive for gear and store?
  Will it be Heaven? Will it be Hell,
    When there is Peace?

This let us pray for, this implore:
That all base dreams thrust out at door,
  We may in loftier aims excel
  And, like men waking from a spell,
Grow stronger, nobler, than before,
    When there is Peace.

Austin Dobson

A PRAYER IN TIME OF WAR

[The war will change many things in art and life, and among them, it is to be hoped, many of our own ideas as to what is, and what is not, "intellectual."]

Thou, whose deep ways are in the sea,
  Whose footsteps are not known,
To-night a world that turned from Thee
  Is waiting—at Thy Throne.

The towering Babels that we raised
  Where scoffing sophists brawl,
The little Antichrists we praised—
  The night is on them all.

The fool hath said . . . The fool hath said . . .
  And we, who deemed him wise,
We who believed that Thou wast dead,
  How should we seek Thine eyes?

How should we seek to Thee for power
  Who scorned Thee yesterday?

How should we kneel, in this dread hour?
Lord, teach us how to pray!

Grant us the single heart, once more,
That mocks no sacred thing,
The Sword of Truth our fathers wore
When Thou wast Lord and King.

Let darkness unto darkness tell
Our deep unspoken prayer,
For, while our souls in darkness dwell,
We know that Thou art there.

Alfred Noyes

THEN AND NOW

When battles were fought
With a chivalrous sense of should and ought,
In spirit men said,
"End we quick or dead,
Honour is some reward!
Let us fight fair—for our own best or worst;
So, Gentlemen of the Guard,
Fire first!"

In the open they stood,
Man to man in his knightlihood:
They would not deign
To profit by a stain
On the honourable rules,
Knowing that practise perfidy no man durst
Who in the heroic schools
Was nurst.

But now, behold, what
Is war with those where honour is not!
Rama laments
Its dead innocents;

Herod howls: "Sly slaughter
Rules now! Let us, by modes once called accurst,
Overhead, under water,
Stab first."

Thomas Hardy

THE KAISER AND GOD

["I rejoice with you in Wilhelm's first victory. How magnificently God supported him!"—Telegram from the Kaiser to the Crown Princess.]

Led by Wilhelm, as you tell,
God has done extremely well;
You with patronizing nod
Show that you approve of God.
Kaiser, face a question new—
This—does God approve of you?

Broken pledges, treaties torn,
Your first page of war adorn;
We on fouler things must look
Who read further in that book,
Where you did in time of war
All that you in peace forswore,
Where you, barbarously wise,
Bade your soldiers terrorize,

Where you made—the deed was fine—
Women screen your firing line.
Villages burned down to dust,
Torture, murder, bestial lust,
Filth too foul for printer's ink,
Crime from which the apes would shrink—
Strange the offerings that you press
On the God of Righteousness!

Kaiser, when you'd decorate
Sons or friends who serve your State,
Not that Iron Cross bestow,
But a cross of wood, and so—
So remind the world that you
Have made Calvary anew.

Kaiser, when you'd kneel in prayer
Look upon your hands, and there
Let that deep and awful stain
From the Wood of children slain
Burn your very soul with shame,
Till you dare not breathe that Name
That now you glibly advertise—
God as one of your allies.

Impious braggart, you forget;
God is not your conscript yet;
You shall learn in dumb amaze
That His ways are not your ways,
That the mire through which you trod
Is not the high white road of God.

To Whom, whichever way the combat rolls,
We, fighting to the end, commend our souls.

Barry Pain

THE SUPERMAN

The horror-haunted Belgian plains riven by shot and shell
Are strewn with her undaunted sons who stayed the jaws of
hell.
In every sunny vale of France death is the countersign.
The purest blood in Britain's veins is being poured like wine.

Far, far across the crimsoned map the impassioned armies
sweep.
Destruction flashes down the sky and penetrates the deep.
The Dreadnought knows the silent dread, and seas incarnadine
Attest the carnival of strife, the madman's battle scene.

Relentless, savage, hot, and grim the infuriate columns press
Where terror simulates disdain and danger is largess,
Where greedy youth claims death for bride and agony seems
bliss.
It is the cause, the cause, my soul! which sanctifies all this.

Ride, Cossacks, ride! Charge, Turcos, charge! The fateful hour
has come.
Let all the guns of Britain roar or be forever dumb.
The Superman has burst his bonds. With Kultur-flag unfurled
And prayer on lip he runs amuck, imperilling the world.

The impious creed that might is right in him personified
Bids all creation bend before the insatiate Teuton pride,
Which, nourished on Valhalla dreams of empire unconfined,
Would make the cannon and the sword the despots of
mankind.

Efficient, thorough, strong, and brave—his vision is to kill.
Force is the hearthstone of his might, the pole-star of his will.
His forges glow malevolent: their minions never tire
To deck the goddess of his lust whose twins are blood and fire.

O world grown sick with butchery and manifold distress!
O broken Belgium robbed of all save grief and ghastliness!
Should Prussian power enslave the world and arrogance
prevail,
Let chaos come, let Moloch rule, and Christ give place to
Baal.

Robert Grant

THREE HILLS

There is a hill in England,
   Green fields and a school I know,
Where the balls fly fast in summer,
   And the whispering elm-trees grow,
         A little hill, a dear hill,
   And the playing fields below.

There is a hill in Flanders,
   Heaped with a thousand slain,
Where the shells fly night and noontide
   And the ghosts that died in vain,—
         A little hill, a hard hill
   To the souls that died in pain.

There is a hill in Jewry,
   Three crosses pierce the sky,
On the midmost He is dying
   To save all those who die,—
         A little hill, a kind hill
   To souls in jeopardy.

Everard Owen
Harrow, December, 1915

THE RETURN

I heard the rumbling guns. I saw the smoke,
   The unintelligible shock of hosts that still,
Far off, unseeing, strove and strove again;
   And Beauty flying naked down the hill

From morn to eve: and the stern night cried Peace!
   And shut the strife in darkness: all was still,
Then slowly crept a triumph on the dark—
   And I heard Beauty singing up the hill.

John Freeman

THE MOBILIZATION IN BRITTANY

I

It was silent in the street.
I did not know until a woman told me,
Sobbing over the muslin she sold me.
Then I went out and walked to the square
And saw a few dazed people standing there.

And then the drums beat, the drums beat!
O then the drums beat!
And hurrying, stumbling through the street
Came the hurrying stumbling feet.
O I have heard the drums beat
For war!
I have heard the townsfolk come,
I have heard the roll and thunder of the nearest drum
As the drummer stopped and cried, "Hear!
Be strong! The summons comes! Prepare!"
Closing he prayed us to be calm . . .

And there was calm in my heart of the desert, of the dead sea,
Of vast plains of the West before the coming storm,
And there was calm in their eyes like the last calm that shall be.

And then the drum beat,
The fatal drum, beat,
And the drummer marched through the street
And down to another square,
And the drummer above took up the beat
And sent it onward where
Huddled, we stood and heard the drums roll,
And then a bell began to toll.

O I have heard the thunder of drums
Crashing into simple poor homes.

I have heard the drums roll "Farewell!"
I have heard the tolling cathedral bell.
Will it ever peal again?
Shall I ever smile or feel again?
What was joy? What was pain?

For I have heard the drums beat,
I have seen the drummer striding from street to street,
Crying, "Be strong! Hear what I must tell!"
While the drums roared and rolled and beat
For war!

II

Last night the men of this region were leaving. Now they are
far.
Rough and strong they are, proud and gay they are.
So this is the way of war . . .

The train was full and we all shouted as it pulled away.
They sang an old war-song, they were true to themselves, they
were gay!
We might have thought they were going for a holiday—

Except for something in the air,
Except for the weeping of the ruddy old women of Finistère.
The younger women do not weep. They dream and stare.

They seem to be walking in dreams. They seem not to know
It is their homes, their happiness, vanishing so.
(Every strong man between twenty and forty must go.)

They sang an old war-song. I have heard it often in other days,
But never before when War was walking the world's highways.
They sang, they shouted, the *Marseillaise!*

The train went and another has gone, but none, coming, has
brought word.
Though you may know, you, out in the world, we have not
heard,
We are not sure that the great battalions have stirred—

Except for something, something in the air,
Except for the weeping of the wild old women of Finistère.
How long will the others dream and stare?

The train went. The strong men of this region are all away,
afar.
Rough and strong they are, proud and gay they are.
So this is the way of war . . .

Grace Fallow Norton

THE TOY BAND

(A SONG OF THE GREAT RETREAT)

Dreary lay the long road, dreary lay the town,
Lights out and never a glint o' moon:
Weary lay the stragglers, half a thousand down,
Sad sighed the weary big Dragoon.
"Oh! if I'd a drum here to make them take the road again,
Oh! if I'd a fife to wheedle, Come, boys, come!
You that mean to fight it out, wake and take your load again,
Fall in! Fall in! Follow the fife and drum!

"Hey, but here's a toy shop, here's a drum for me,
Penny whistles too to play the tune!
Half a thousand dead men soon shall hear and see
We're a band!" said the weary big Dragoon.
"Rubadub! Rubadub! Wake and take the road again,
Wheedle-deedle-deedle-dee, Come, boys, come!
You that mean to fight it out, wake and take your load again,
Fall in! Fall in! Follow the fife and drum!"

Cheerly goes the dark road, cheerly goes the night,
    Cheerly goes the blood to keep the beat:
Half a thousand dead men marching on to fight
    With a little penny drum to lift their feet.
Rubadub! Rubadub! Wake and take the road again,
    Wheedle-deedle-deedle-dee, Come, boys, come!
You that mean to fight it out, wake and take your load again,
    Fall in! Fall in! Follow the fife and drum!

As long as there's an Englishman to ask a tale of me,
    As long as I can tell the tale aright,
We'll not forget the penny whistle's wheedle-deedle-dee
    And the big Dragoon a-beating down the night,
Rubadub! Rubadub! Wake and take the road again,
    Wheedle-deedle-deedle-dee, Come, boys, come!
You that mean to fight it out, wake and take your load again,
    Fall in! Fall in! Follow the fife and drum!

Henry Newbolt

THOMAS OF THE LIGHT HEART

Facing the guns, he jokes as well
        As any Judge upon the Bench;
Between the crash of shell and shell
        His laughter rings along the trench;
He seems immensely tickled by a
Projectile which he calls a "Black Maria."

He whistles down the day-long road,
        And, when the chilly shadows fall
And heavier hangs the weary load,
        Is he down-hearted? Not at all.
'T is then he takes a light and airy
View of the tedious route to Tipperary.

His songs are not exactly hymns;
        He never learned them in the choir;
And yet they brace his dragging limbs

Although they miss the sacred fire;
Although his choice and cherished gems
Do not include "The Watch upon the Thames."

He takes to fighting as a game;
He does no talking, through his hat,
Of holy missions; all the same
He has his faith—be sure of that;
He'll not disgrace his sporting breed,
Nor play what isn't cricket. There's his creed.

Owen Seaman
October, 1914

IN THE TRENCHES

As I lay in the trenches
Under the Hunter's Moon,
My mind ran to the lenches
Cut in a Wiltshire down.

I saw their long black shadows,
The beeches in the lane,
The gray church in the meadows
And my white cottage—plain.

Thinks I, the down lies dreaming
Under that hot moon's eye,
Which sees the shells fly screaming
And men and horses die.

And what makes she, I wonder,
Of the horror and the blood,
And what's her luck, to sunder
The evil from the good?

'T was more than I could compass,
For how was I to think

With such infernal rumpus
In such a blasted stink?

But here's a thought to tally
With t'other. That moon sees
A shrouded German valley
With woods and ghostly trees.

And maybe there's a river
As we have got at home
With poplar-trees aquiver
And clots of whirling foam.

And over there some fellow,
A German and a foe,
Whose gills are turning yellow
As sure as mine are so,

Watches that riding glory
Apparel'd in her gold,
And craves to hear the story
Her frozen lips enfold.

And if he sees as clearly
As I do where her shrine
Must fall, he longs as dearly.
With heart as full as mine.

Maurice Hewlett

THE GUARDS CAME THROUGH

Men of the Twenty-first
    Up by the Chalk Pit Wood,
Weak with our wounds and our thirst,
    Wanting our sleep and our food,
After a day and a night—
    God, shall we ever forget!
Beaten and broke in the fight,

But sticking it—sticking it yet.
Trying to hold the line,
Fainting and spent and done,
Always the thud and the whine,
Always the yell of the Hun!
Northumberland, Lancaster, York,
Durham and Somerset,
Fighting alone, worn to the bone,
But sticking it—sticking it yet.

Never a message of hope!
Never a word of cheer!
Fronting Hill 70's shell-swept slope,
With the dull dead plain in our rear.
Always the whine of the shell,
Always the roar of its burst,
Always the tortures of hell,
As waiting and wincing we cursed
Our luck and the guns and the *Boche*,
When our Corporal shouted, "Stand to!"
And I heard some one cry, "Clear the front for the Guards!"
And the Guards came through.

Our throats they were parched and hot,
But Lord, if you'd heard the cheers!
Irish and Welsh and Scot,
Coldstream and Grenadiers.
Two brigades, if you please,
Dressing as straight as a hem,
We—we were down on our knees,
Praying for us and for them!
Lord, I could speak for a week,
But how could you understand!
How should *your* cheeks be wet,
Such feelin's don't come to *you*.
But when can me or my mates forget,
When the Guards came through?

“Five yards left extend!”
    It passed from rank to rank.
Line after line with never a bend,
    And a touch of the London swank.
A trifle of swank and dash,
    Cool as a home parade,
Twinkle and glitter and flash,
    Flinching never a shade,
With the shrapnel right in their face
    Doing their Hyde Park stunt,
Keeping their swing at an easy pace,
    Arms at the trail, eyes front!
Man, it was great to see!
    Man, it was fine to do!
It’s a cot and a hospital ward for me,
But I’ll tell ‘em in Blighty, wherever I be,
    How the Guards came through.

Arthur Conan Doyle

THE PASSENGERS OF A RETARDED SUBMERSIBLE

NOVEMBER, 1916

THE AMERICAN PEOPLE:

What was it kept you so long, brave German submersible?
We have been very anxious lest matters had not gone well
With you and the precious cargo of your country’s drugs and
    dyes.
But here you are at last, and the sight is good for our eyes,
Glad to welcome you up and out of the caves of the sea,
And ready for sale or barter, whatever your will may be.

THE CAPTAIN OF THE SUBMERSIBLE:

Oh, do not be impatient, good friends of this neutral land,
That we have been so tardy in reaching your eager strand.
We were stopped by a curious chance just off the Irish coast,
Where the mightiest wreck ever was lay crowded with a host

Of the dead that went down with her; and some prayed us to bring them here
That they might be at home with their brothers and sisters dear.
We Germans have tender hearts, and it grieved us sore to say
We were not a passenger ship, and to most we must answer nay,
But if from among their hundreds they could somehow a half-score choose
We thought we could manage to bring them, and we would not refuse.
They chose, and the women and children that are greeting you here are those
Ghosts of the women and children that the rest of the hundred chose.

THE AMERICAN PEOPLE:

What guff are you giving us, Captain? We are able to tell, we hope,
A dozen ghosts, when we see them, apart from a periscope.
Come, come, get down to business! For time is money, you know,
And you must make up in both to us for having been so slow.
Better tell this story of yours to the submarines, for we
Know there was no such wreck, and none of your spookery.

THE GHOSTS OF THE LUSITANIA WOMEN AND CHILDREN:

Oh, kind kin of our murderers, take us back when you sail away;
Our own kin have forgotten us. O Captain, do not stay!
But hasten, Captain, hasten: The wreck that lies under the sea
Shall be ever the home for us this land can never be.

William Dean Howells

EDITH CAVELL

She was binding the wounds of her enemies when they
came—
The lint in her hand unrolled.
They battered the door with their rifle-butts, crashed it in:
She faced them gentle and bold.

They haled her before the judges where they sat
In their places, helmet on head.
With question and menace the judges assailed her, "Yes,
I have broken your law," she said.

"I have tended the hurt and hidden the hunted, have done
As a sister does to a brother,
Because of a law that is greater than that you have made,
Because I could do none other.

"Deal as you will with me. This is my choice to the end,
To live in the life I vowed."
"She is self-confessed," they cried; "she is self-condemned.
She shall die, that the rest may be cowed."

In the terrible hour of the dawn, when the veins are cold,
They led her forth to the wall.
"I have loved my land," she said, "but it is not enough:
Love requires of me all.

"I will empty my heart of the bitterness, hating none."
And sweetness filled her brave
With a vision of understanding beyond the hour
That knelled to the waiting grave.

They bound her eyes, but she stood as if she shone.
The rifles it was that shook
When the hoarse command rang out. They could not endure
That last, that defenceless look.

And the officer strode and pistolled her surely, ashamed
That men, seasoned in blood,
Should quail at a woman, only a woman,—
As a flower stamped in the mud.

And now that the deed was securely done, in the night
When none had known her fate,
They answered those that had striven for her, day by day:
"It is over, you come too late."

And with many words and sorrowful-phrased excuse
Argued their German right
To kill, most legally; hard though the duty be,
The law must assert its might.

Only a woman! yet she had pity on them,
The victim offered slain
To the gods of fear that they worship. Leave them there,
Red hands, to clutch their gain!

She bewailed not herself, and we will bewail her not,
But with tears of pride rejoice
That an English soul was found so crystal-clear
To be triumphant voice

Of the human heart that dares adventure all
But live to itself untrue,
And beyond all laws sees love as the light in the night,
As the star it must answer to.

The hurts she healed, the thousands comforted—these
Make a fragrance of her fame.
But because she stept to her star right on through death
It is Victory speaks her name.

Laurence Binyon

THE HELL-GATE OF SOISSONS

My name is Darino, the poet. You have heard? *Oui, Comédie Française.*
Perchance it has happened, *mon ami*, you know of my unworthy lays.
Ah, then you must guess how my fingers are itching to talk to a pen;
For I was at Soissons, and saw it, the death of the twelve Englishmen.

My leg, *malheureusement*, I left it behind on the banks of the Aisne.
Regret? I would pay with the other to witness their valor again.
A trifle, indeed, I assure you, to give for the honor to tell
How that handful of British, undaunted, went into the Gateway of Hell.

Let me draw you a plan of the battle. Here we French and your Engineers stood;
Over there a detachment of German sharpshooters lay hid in a wood.
A *mitrailleuse* battery planted on top of this well-chosen ridge
Held the road for the Prussians and covered the direct approach to the bridge.

It was madness to dare the dense murder that spewed from those ghastly machines.
(Only those who have danced to its music can know what the
mitrailleuse means.)
But the bridge on the Aisne was a menace; our safety demanded its fall:
"Engineers,—volunteers!" In a body, the Royals stood out at the call.

Death at best was the fate of that mission—to their glory not one was dismayed.
A party was chosen—and seven survived till the powder was laid.
And *they* died with their fuses unlighted. Another detachment! Again
A sortie is made—all too vainly. The bridge still commanded the Aisne.

We were fighting two foes—Time and Prussia—the moments were worth more than troops.
We *must* blow up the bridge. A lone soldier darts out from the Royals and swoops
For the fuse! Fate seems with us. We cheer him; he answers—our hopes are reborn!
A ball rips his visor—his khaki shows red where another has torn.

Will he live—will he last—will he make it? *Hélas!* And so near to the goal!
A second, he dies! then a third one! A fourth! Still the Germans take toll!
A fifth, *magnifique*! It is magic! How does he escape them? He may . . .
Yes, he *does*! See, the match flares! A rifle rings out from the wood and says "Nay!"

Six, seven, eight, nine take their places, six, seven, eight, nine brave their hail;
Six, seven, eight, nine—how we count them! But the sixth, seventh, eighth, and ninth fail!
A tenth! *Sacré nom!* But these English are soldiers—they know how to try;
(He fumbles the place where his jaw was)—they show, too, how heroes can die.

Ten we count—ten who ventured unquailing—ten there were—and ten are no more!
Yet another salutes and superbly essays where the ten failed before.
God of Battles, look down and protect him! Lord, his heart is as Thine—let him live!
But the *mitrailleuse* splutters and stutters, and riddles him into a sieve.

Then I thought of my sins, and sat waiting the charge that we could not withstand.
And I thought of my beautiful Paris, and gave a last look at the land,

At France, my *belle France*, in her glory of blue sky and green field
and wood.
Death with honor, but never surrender. And to die with such
men—it was good.

They are forming—the bugles are blaring—they will cross in a
moment and then . . .
When out of the line of the Royals (your island, *mon ami*, breeds
men)
Burst a private, a tawny-haired giant—it was hopeless, but, *ciel!* how
he ran!
Bon Dieu please remember the pattern, and make many more on
his plan!

No cheers from our ranks, and the Germans, they halted in
wonderment too;
See, he reaches the bridge; ah! he lights it! I am dreaming, it *cannot*
be true.
Screams of rage! *Fusillade!* They have killed him! Too late though,
the good work is done.
By the valor of twelve English martyrs, the Hell-Gate of Soissons
is won!

Herbert Kaufman

THE VIRGIN OF ALBERT

(NOTRE DAME DE BREBIÈRES)

Shyly expectant, gazing up at Her,
They linger, Gaul and Briton, side by side:
Death they know well, for daily have they died,
Spending their boyhood ever bravelier;
They wait: here is no priest or chorister,
Birds skirt the stricken tower, terrified;
Desolate, empty, is the Eastertide,
Yet still they wait, watching the Babe and Her.

Broken, the Mother stoops: the brutish foe
  Hurled with dull hate his bolts, and down She swayed,
Down, till She saw the toiling swarms below,—
  Platoons, guns, transports, endlessly arrayed:
"Women are woe for them! let Me be theirs,
And comfort them, and hearken all their prayers!"

George Herbert Clarke

RETREAT

Broken, bewildered by the long retreat
  Across the stifling leagues of southern plain,
  Across the scorching leagues of trampled grain,
Half-stunned, half-blinded, by the trudge of feet
And dusty smother of the August heat,
  He dreamt of flowers in an English lane,
  Of hedgerow flowers glistening after rain—
All-heal and willow-herb and meadow-sweet.

All-heal and willow-herb and meadow-sweet—
  The innocent names kept up a cool refrain—
All-heal and willow-herb and meadow-sweet,
  Chiming and tinkling in his aching brain,
  Until he babbled like a child again—
"All-heal and willow-herb and meadow-sweet."

Wilfrid Wilson Gibson

A LETTER FROM THE FRONT

I was out early to-day, spying about
From the top of a haystack—such a lovely morning—
And when I mounted again to canter back
I saw across a field in the broad sunlight
A young Gunner Subaltern, stalking along
With a rook-rifle held at the ready, and—would you believe
  it?—
A domestic cat, soberly marching beside him.

So I laughed, and felt quite well disposed to the youngster,
And shouted out "the top of the morning" to him,
And wished him "Good sport!"—and then I remembered
My rank, and his, and what I ought to be doing:
And I rode nearer, and added, "I can only suppose
You have not seen the Commander-in-Chief's order
Forbidding English officers to annoy their Allies
By hunting and shooting."

But he stood and saluted
And said earnestly, "I beg your pardon, Sir,
I was only going out to shoot a sparrow
To feed my cat with."

So there was the whole picture,
The lovely early morning, the occasional shell
Screeching and scattering past us, the empty landscape,—
Empty, except for the young Gunner saluting,
And the cat, anxiously watching his every movement.

I may be wrong, and I may have told it badly,
But it struck *me* as being extremely ludicrous.

Henry Newbolt

RHEIMS CATHEDRAL—1914

A wingèd death has smitten dumb thy bells,
And poured them molten from thy tragic towers:
Now are the windows dust that were thy flower
Patterned like frost, petalled like asphodels.
Gone are the angels and the archangels,
The saints, the little lamb above thy door,
The shepherd Christ! They are not, any more,
Save in the soul where exiled beauty dwells.

But who has heard within thy vaulted gloom
That old divine insistence of the sea,
When music flows along the sculptured stone
In tides of prayer, for him thy windows bloom

Like faithful sunset, warm immortally!
    Thy bells live on, and Heaven is in their tone!

Grace Hazard Conkling

I HAVE A RENDEZVOUS WITH DEATH . . .

I have a rendezvous with Death
At some disputed barricade,
When Spring comes back with rustling shade
And apple-blossoms fill the air—
I have a rendezvous with Death
When Spring brings back blue days and fair.

It may be he shall take my hand
And lead me into his dark land
And close my eyes and quench my breath—
It may be I shall pass him still.
I have a rendezvous with Death
On some scarred slope of battered hill,
When Spring comes round again this year
And the first meadow-flowers appear.

God knows 't were better to be deep
Pillowed in silk and scented down,
Where Love throbs out in blissful sleep
Pulse nigh to pulse, and breath to breath,
Where hushed awakenings are dear . . .
But I've a rendezvous with Death
At midnight in some flaming town,
When Spring trips north again this year,
And I to my pledged word am true,
I shall not fail that rendezvous.

Alan Seeger

THE SOLDIER

If I should die, think only this of me:
    That there's some corner of a foreign field
That is for ever England. There shall be
    In that rich earth a richer dust concealed;
A dust whom England bore, shaped, made aware,
    Gave once her flowers to love, her ways to roam,
A body of England's, breathing English air,
    Washed by the rivers, blest by suns of home.

And think this heart, all evil shed away,
    A pulse in the eternal mind, no less
        Gives somewhere back the thoughts by England given;
Her sights and sounds; dreams happy as her day;
    And laughter, learnt of friends; and gentleness,
        In hearts at peace, under an English heaven.

Rupert Brooke

EXPECTANS EXPECTAVI

From morn to midnight, all day through,
I laugh and play as others do,
I sin and chatter, just the same
As others with a different name.

And all year long upon the stage,
I dance and tumble and do rage
So vehemently, I scarcely see
The inner and eternal me.

I have a temple I do not
Visit, a heart I have forgot,
A self that I have never met,
A secret shrine—and yet, and yet

This sanctuary of my soul
Unwitting I keep white and whole,

Unlatched and lit, if Thou should'st care
To enter or to tarry there.

With parted lips and outstretched hands
And listening ears Thy servant stands,
Call Thou early, call Thou late,
To Thy great service dedicate.

Charles Hamilton Sorley
May, 1915

THE VOLUNTEER

Here lies a clerk who half his life had spent
Toiling at ledgers in a city grey,
Thinking that so his days would drift away
With no lance broken in life's tournament:
Yet ever 'twixt the books and his bright eyes
The gleaming eagles of the legions came,
And horsemen, charging under phantom skies,
Went thundering past beneath the oriflamme.

And now those waiting dreams are satisfied;
From twilight to the halls of dawn he went;
His lance is broken; but he lies content
With that high hour, in which he lived and died.
And falling thus he wants no recompense,
Who found his battle in the last resort;
Nor needs he any hearse to bear him hence,
Who goes to join the men of Agincourt.

Herbert Asquith

INTO BATTLE

The naked earth is warm with Spring,
    And with green grass and bursting trees
Leans to the sun's gaze glorying,
    And quivers in the sunny breeze;

And Life is Colour and Warmth and Light,
  And a striving evermore for these;
And he is dead who will not fight;
  And who dies fighting has increase.

The fighting man shall from the sun
  Take warmth, and life from the glowing earth;
Speed with the light-foot winds to run,
  And with the trees to newer birth;
And find, when fighting shall be done,
  Great rest, and fullness after dearth.

All the bright company of Heaven
  Hold him in their high comradeship,
The Dog-Star, and the Sisters Seven,
  Orion's Belt and sworded hip.

The woodland trees that stand together,
  They stand to him each one a friend;
They gently speak in the windy weather;
  They guide to valley and ridges' end.

The kestrel hovering by day,
  And the little owls that call by night,
Bid him be swift and keen as they,
  As keen of ear, as swift of sight.

The blackbird sings to him, "Brother, brother,
  If this be the last song you shall sing,
Sing well, for you may not sing another;
  Brother, sing."

In dreary, doubtful, waiting hours,
  Before the brazen frenzy starts,
The horses show him nobler powers;
  O patient eyes, courageous hearts!

And when the burning moment breaks,
  And all things else are out of mind,

And only Joy-of-Battle takes
  Him by the throat, and makes him blind,

Through joy and blindness he shall know,
  Not caring much to know, that still
Nor lead nor steel shall reach him, so
  That it be not the Destined Will.

The thundering line of battle stands,
  And in the air Death moans and sings;
But Day shall clasp him with strong hands,
  And Night shall fold him in soft wings.

Julian Grenfell
Flanders, April, 1915

THE CRICKETERS OF FLANDERS

The first to climb the parapet
With "cricket balls" in either hand;
The first to vanish in the smoke
Of God-forsaken No Man's Land;
First at the wire and soonest through,
First at those red-mouthed hounds of hell,
The Maxims, and the first to fall,—
They do their bit and do it well.

Full sixty yards I've seen them throw
With all that nicety of aim
They learned on British cricket-fields.
Ah, bombing is a Briton's game!
Shell-hole to shell-hole, trench, to trench,
"Lobbing them over" with an eye
As true as though it *were* a game
And friends were having tea close by.

Pull down some art-offending thing
Of carven stone, and in its stead
Let splendid bronze commemorate

These men, the living and the dead.
No figure of heroic size,
Towering skyward like a god;
But just a lad who might have stepped
From any British bombing squad.

His shrapnel helmet set atilt,
His bombing waistcoat sagging low,
His rifle slung across his back:
Poised in the very act to throw.
And let some graven legend tell
Of those weird battles in the West
Wherein he put old skill to use,
And played old games with sterner zest.

Thus should he stand, reminding those
In less-believing days, perchance,
How Britain's fighting cricketers
Helped bomb the Germans out of France.
And other eyes than ours would see;
And other hearts than ours would thrill;
And others say, as we have said:
"A sportsman and a soldier still!"

James Norman Hall

"ALL THE HILLS AND VALES ALONG"

All the hills and vales along
Earth is bursting into song,
And the singers are the chaps
Who are going to die perhaps.
    O sing, marching men,
    Till the valleys ring again.
    Give your gladness to earth's keeping,
    So be glad, when you are sleeping.

Cast away regret and rue,
Think what you are marching to.

Little live, great pass.
Jesus Christ and Barabbas
Were found the same day.
This died, that went his way.
  So sing with joyful breath.
  For why, you are going to death.
  Teeming earth will surely store
  All the gladness that you pour.

Earth that never doubts nor fears,
Earth that knows of death, not tears,
Earth that bore with joyful ease
Hemlock for Socrates,
Earth that blossomed and was glad
'Neath the cross that Christ had,
Shall rejoice and blossom too
When the bullet reaches you.
  Wherefore, men marching
  On the road to death, sing!
  Pour your gladness on earth's head,
  So be merry, so be dead.

From the hills and valleys earth.
Shouts back the sound of mirth,
Tramp of feet and lilt of song
Ringing all the road along.
All the music of their going,
Ringing, swinging, glad song-throwing,
Earth will echo still, when foot
Lies numb and voice mute.
  On, marching men, on
  To the gates of death with song.
  Sow your gladness for earth's reaping,
  So you may be glad, though sleeping.
  Strew your gladness on earth's bed,
  So be merry, so be dead.

Charles Hamilton Sorley

NO MAN'S LAND

No Man's Land is an eerie sight
At early dawn in the pale gray light.
Never a house and never a hedge
In No Man's Land from edge to edge,
And never a living soul walks there
To taste the fresh of the morning air;—
Only some lumps of rotting clay,
That were friends or foemen yesterday.

What are the bounds of No Man's Land?
You can see them clearly on either hand,
A mound of rag-bags gray in the sun,
Or a furrow of brown where the earthworks run
From the eastern hills to the western sea,
Through field or forest o'er river and lea;
No man may pass them, but aim you well
And Death rides across on the bullet or shell.

But No Man's Land is a goblin sight
When patrols crawl over at dead o' night;
Boche or British, Belgian or French,
You dice with death when you cross the trench.
When the "rapid," like fireflies in the dark,
Flits down the parapet spark by spark,
And you drop for cover to keep your head
With your face on the breast of the four months' dead.

The man who ranges in No Man's Land
Is dogged by the shadows on either hand
When the star-shell's flare, as it bursts o'erhead,
Scares the gray rats that feed on the dead,
And the bursting bomb or the bayonet-snatch
May answer the click of your safety-catch,
For the lone patrol, with his life in his hand,
Is hunting for blood in No Man's Land.

James H. Knight-Adkin

CHAMPAGNE, 1914-15

In the glad revels, in the happy fêtes,
  When cheeks are flushed, and glasses gilt and pearled
With the sweet wine of France that concentrates
  The sunshine and the beauty of the world,

Drink sometimes, you whose footsteps yet may tread
  The undisturbed, delightful paths of Earth,
To those whose blood, in pious duty shed,
  Hallows the soil where that same wine had birth.

Here, by devoted comrades laid away,
  Along our lines they slumber where they fell,
Beside the crater at the Ferme d'Alger
  And up the bloody slopes of La Pompelle,

And round the city whose cathedral towers
  The enemies of Beauty dared profane,
And in the mat of multicolored flowers
  That clothe the sunny chalk-fields of Champagne,

Under the little crosses where they rise
  The soldier rests. Now round him undismayed
The cannon thunders, and at night he lies
  At peace beneath the eternal fusillade . . .

That other generations might possess—
  From shame and menace free in years to come—
A richer heritage of happiness,
  He marched to that heroic martyrdom.

Esteeming less the forfeit that he paid
  Than undishonored that his flag might float
Over the towers of liberty, he made
  His breast the bulwark and his blood the moat.

Obscurely sacrificed, his nameless tomb,
  Bare of the sculptor's art, the poet's lines,

Summer shall flush with poppy-fields in bloom,
    And Autumn yellow with maturing vines.

There the grape-pickers at their harvesting
    Shall lightly tread and load their wicker trays,
Blessing his memory as they toil and sing
    In the slant sunshine of October days . . .

I love to think that if my blood should be
    So privileged to sink where his has sunk,
I shall not pass from Earth entirely,
    But when the banquet rings, when healths are drunk,

And faces that the joys of living fill
    Glow radiant with laughter and good cheer,
In beaming cups some spark of me shall still
    Brim toward the lips that once I held so dear.

So shall one coveting no higher plane
    Than nature clothes in color and flesh and tone,
Even from the grave put upward to attain
    The dreams youth cherished and missed and might have known;

And that strong need that strove unsatisfied
    Toward earthly beauty in all forms it wore,
Not death itself shall utterly divide
    From the beloved shapes it thirsted for.

Alas, how many an adept for whose arms
    Life held delicious offerings perished here,
How many in the prime of all that charms,
    Crowned with all gifts that conquer and endear!

Honor them not so much with tears and flowers,
    But you with whom the sweet fulfilment lies,
Where in the anguish of atrocious hours
    Turned their last thoughts and closed their dying eyes,

Rather when music on bright gatherings lays
Its tender spell, and joy is uppermost,
Be mindful of the men they were, and raise
Your glasses to them in one silent toast.

Drink to them—amorous of dear Earth as well,
They asked no tribute lovelier than this—
And in the wine that ripened where they fell,
Oh, frame your lips as though it were a kiss.

Alan Seeger
Champagne, France,
July, 1915

HEADQUARTERS

A league and a league from the trenches—from the traversed maze of the lines,
Where daylong the sniper watches and daylong the bullet whines,
And the cratered earth is in travail with mines and with countermines—
Here, where haply some woman dreamed (are those her roses that bloom
In the garden beyond the windows of my littered working room?)
We have decked the map for our masters as a bride is decked for the groom.

Fair, on each lettered numbered square—crossroad and mound and wire,
Loophole, redoubt, and emplacement—lie the targets their mouths desire;
Gay with purples and browns and blues, have we traced them their arcs of fire.

And ever the type-keys chatter; and ever our keen wires bring
Word from the watchers a-crouch below, word from

the watchers a-wing:
And ever we hear the distant growl of our hid 'guns
thundering.

Hear it hardly, and turn again to our maps, where the
trench lines crawl,
Red on the gray and each with a sign for the ranging
shrapnel's fall—
Snakes that our masters shall scotch at dawn, as is
written here on the wall.

For the weeks of our waiting draw to a close . . .
There is scarcely a leaf astir
In the garden beyond my windows, where the twilight
shadows blur
The blaze of some woman's roses . . . "Bombardment
orders, sir."

Gilbert Frankau

HOME THOUGHTS FROM LAVENTIE

Green gardens in Laventie!
Soldiers only know the street
Where the mud is churned and splashed about
By battle-wending feet;
And yet beside one stricken house there is a glimpse of
grass—
Look for it when you pass.

Beyond the church whose pitted spire
Seems balanced on a strand
Of swaying stone and tottering brick,
Two roofless ruins stand;
And here, among the wreckage, where the back-wall should
have been,
We found a garden green.

The grass was never trodden on,
The little path of gravel
Was overgrown with celandine;
        No other folk did travel
Along its weedy surface but the nimble-footed mouse,
        Running from house to house.

So all along the tender blades
Of soft and vivid grass
We lay, nor heard the limber wheels
        That pass and ever pass
In noisy continuity until their stony rattle
        Seems in itself a battle.

At length we rose up from this ease
Of tranquil happy mind,
And searched the garden's little length
        Some new pleasaunce to find;
And there some yellow daffodils, and jasmine hanging high,
        Did rest the tired eye.

The fairest and most fragrant
Of the many sweets we found
Was a little bush of Daphne flower
        Upon a mossy mound,
And so thick were the blossoms set and so divine the scent,
        That we were well content.

Hungry for Spring I bent my head,
The perfume fanned my face,
And all my soul was dancing
        In that lovely little place,
Dancing with a measured step from wrecked and shattered
    towns
        Away . . . upon the Downs.

I saw green banks of daffodil,
Slim poplars in the breeze,
Great tan-brown hares in gusty March

A-courting on the leas.
And meadows, with their glittering streams—and silver-scurrying dace—
Home, what a perfect place!

E. Wyndham Tennant

A PETITION

All that a man might ask thou hast given me, England,
Birthright and happy childhood's long heart's-ease,
And love whose range is deep beyond all sounding
And wider than all seas:
A heart to front the world and find God in it.
Eyes blind enow but not too blind to see
The lovely things behind the dross and darkness,
And lovelier things to be;
And friends whose loyalty time nor death shall weaken
And quenchless hope and laughter's golden store—
All that a man might ask thou hast given me, England,
Yet grant thou one thing more:
That now when envious foes would spoil thy splendour,
Unversed in arms, a dreamer such, as I,
May in thy ranks be deemed not all unworthy,
England, for thee to die.

Robert Ernest Vernède

FULFILMENT

Was there love once? I have forgotten her.
Was there grief once? Grief yet is mine.
Other loves I have, men rough, but men who stir
More grief, more joy, than love of thee and thine.

Faces cheerful, full of whimsical mirth,
Lined by the wind, burned by the sun;
Bodies enraptured by the abounding earth,
As whose children we are brethren: one.

And any moment may descend hot death
To shatter limbs! Pulp, tear, blast
Belovèd soldiers who love rough life and breath
Not less for dying faithful to the last.

O the fading eyes, the grimed face turned bony,
Oped mouth gushing, fallen head,
Lessening pressure of a hand, shrunk, clammed and stony!
O sudden spasm, release of the dead!

Was there love once? I have forgotten her.
Was there grief once? Grief yet is mine.
O loved, living, dying, heroic soldier,
All, all my joy, my grief, my love, are thine.

Robert Nichols

THE DAY'S MARCH

The battery grides and jingles,
Mile succeeds to mile;
Shaking the noonday sunshine
The guns lunge out awhile,
And then are still awhile.

We amble along the highway;
The reeking, powdery dust
Ascends and cakes our faces
With a striped, sweaty crust.

Under the still sky's violet
The heat throbs on the air . . .
The white road's dusty radiance
Assumes a dark glare.

With a head hot and heavy,
And eyes that cannot rest,
And a black heart burning
In a stifled breast,

I sit in the saddle,
I feel the road unroll,
And keep my senses straightened
Toward to-morrow's goal.

There, over unknown meadows
Which we must reach at last,
Day and night thunders
A black and chilly blast.

Heads forget heaviness,
Hearts forget spleen,
For by that mighty winnowing
Being is blown clean.

Light in the eyes again,
Strength in the hand,
A spirit dares, dies, forgives,
And can understand!

And, best! Love comes back again
After grief and shame,
And along the wind of death
Throws a clean flame.

* * * * *

The battery grides and jingles,
Mile succeeds to mile;
Suddenly battering the silence
The guns burst out awhile . . .

I lift my head and smile.

Robert Nichols

THE SIGN

We are here in a wood of little beeches:
And the leaves are like black lace
Against a sky of nacre.

One bough of clear promise
Across the moon.

It is in this wise that God speaketh unto me.
He layeth hands of healing upon my flesh,
Stilling it in an eternal peace,
Until my soul reaches out myriad and infinite hands
Toward him,
And is eased of its hunger.

And I know that this passes:
This implacable fury and torment of men,
As a thing insensate and vain:
And the stillness hath said unto me,
Over the tumult of sounds and shaken flame,
Out of the terrible beauty of wrath,
I alone am eternal.

One bough of clear promise
Across the moon.

Frederic Manning

THE TRENCHES

Endless lanes sunken in the clay,
Bays, and traverses, fringed with wasted herbage,
Seed-pods of blue scabious, and some lingering blooms;
And the sky, seen as from a well,
Brilliant with frosty stars.
We stumble, cursing, on the slippery duck-boards.
Goaded like the damned by some invisible wrath,

A will stronger than weariness, stronger than animal fear,
Implacable and monotonous.

Here a shaft, slanting, and below
A dusty and flickering light from one feeble candle
And prone figures sleeping uneasily,
Murmuring,
And men who cannot sleep,
With faces impassive as masks,
Bright, feverish eyes, and drawn lips,
Sad, pitiless, terrible faces,
Each an incarnate curse.

Here in a bay, a helmeted sentry
Silent and motionless, watching while two sleep,
And he sees before him
With indifferent eyes the blasted and torn land
Peopled with stiff prone forms, stupidly rigid,
As tho' they had not been men.

Dead are the lips where love laughed or sang,
The hands of youth eager to lay hold of life,
Eyes that have laughed to eyes,
And these were begotten,
O Love, and lived lightly, and burnt
With the lust of a man's first strength: ere they were rent.
Almost at unawares, savagely; and strewn
In bloody fragments, to be the carrion
Of rats and crows.

And the sentry moves not, searching
Night for menace with weary eyes.

Frederic Manning

SONNETS

I

I see across the chasm of flying years
  The pyre of Dido on the vacant shore;
  I see Medea's fury and hear the roar
Of rushing flames, the new bride's burning tears;
And ever as still another vision peers
  Thro' memory's mist to stir me more and more,
  I say that surely I have lived before
And known this joy and trembled with these fears.

The passion that they show me burns so high;
  Their love, in me who have not looked on love,
  So fiercely flames; so wildly comes the cry
Of stricken women the warrior's call above,
That I would gladly lay me down and die
  To wake again where Helen and Hector move.

II

The falling rain is music overhead,
  The dark night, lit by no Intruding star,
  Fit covering yields to thoughts that roam afar
And turn again familiar paths to tread,
Where many a laden hour too quickly sped
  In happier times, before the dawn of war,
  Before the spoiler had whet his sword to mar
The faithful living and the mighty dead.

It is not that my soul is weighed with woe,
  But rather wonder, seeing they do but sleep.
  As birds that in the sinking summer sweep
Across the heaven to happier climes to go,
  So they are gone; and sometimes we must weep,
And sometimes, smiling, murmur, "Be it so!"

Henry William Hutchinson

THE MESSINES ROAD

I

The road that runs up to Messines
　Is double-locked with gates of fire,
Barred with high ramparts, and between
　The unbridged river, and the wire.

None ever goes up to Messines,
　For Death lurks all about the town,
Death holds the vale as his demesne,
　And only Death moves up and down.

II

Choked with wild weeds, and overgrown
　With rank grass, all torn and rent
By war's opposing engines, strewn
　With débris from each day's event!

And in the dark the broken trees,
　Whose arching boughs were once its shade,
Grim and distorted, ghostly ease
　In groans their souls vexed and afraid.

Yet here the farmer drove his cart,
　Here friendly folk would meet and pass,
Here bore the good wife eggs to mart
　And old and young walked up to Mass.

Here schoolboys lingered in the way,
　Here the bent packman laboured by,
And lovers at the end o' the day
　Whispered their secret blushingly.

A goodly road for simple needs,
　An avenue to praise and paint,

Kept by fair use from wreck and weeds,
    Blessed by the shrine of its own saint.

III

The road that runs up to Messines!
    Ah, how we guard it day and night!
And how they guard it, who o'erween
    A stricken people, with their might!

But we shall go up to Messines
    Even thro' that fire-defended gate.
Over and thro' all else between
    And give the highway back its state.

J. E. Stewart

THE CHALLENGE OF THE GUNS

By day, by night, along the lines their dull boom rings,
And that reverberating roar its challenge flings.
Not only unto thee across the narrow sea,
But from the loneliest vale in the last land's heart
The sad-eyed watching mother sees her sons depart.

And freighted full the tumbling waters of ocean are
With aid for England from England's sons afar.
The glass is dim; we see not wisely, far, nor well,
But bred of English bone, and reared on Freedom's wine,
All that we have and are we lay on England's shrine.

A. N. Field

THE BEACH ROAD BY THE WOOD

I know a beach road,
    A road where I would go,
It runs up northward
    From Cooden Bay to Hoe;

And there, in the High Woods,
Daffodils grow.

And whoever walks along there
Stops short and sees,
By the moist tree-roots
In a clearing of the trees,
Yellow great battalions of them,
Blowing in the breeze.

While the spring sun brightens,
And the dull sky clears,
They blow their golden trumpets,
Those golden trumpeteers!
They blow their golden trumpets
And they shake their glancing spears.

And all the rocking beech-trees
Are bright with buds again,
And the green and open spaces
Are greener after rain,
And far to southward one can hear
The sullen, moaning rain.

Once before I die
I will leave the town behind,
The loud town, the dark town
That cramps and chills the mind,
And I'll stand again bareheaded there
In the sunlight and the wind.

Yes, I shall stand
Where as a boy I stood
Above the dykes and levels
In the beach road by the wood,
And I'll smell again the sea breeze,
Salt and harsh and good.

And there shall rise to me
    From that consecrated ground
The old dreams, the lost dreams
    That years and cares have drowned;
Welling up within me
    And above me and around
The song that I could never sing
    And the face I never found.

Geoffrey Howard

GERMAN PRISONERS

When first I saw you in the curious street
Like some platoon of soldier ghosts in grey,
My mad impulse was all to smite and slay,
To spit upon you—tread you 'neath my feet.
But when I saw how each sad soul did greet
My gaze with no sign of defiant frown,
How from tired eyes looked spirits broken down,
How each face showed the pale flag of defeat,
And doubt, despair, and disillusionment,
And how were grievous wounds on many a head.
And on your garb red-faced was other red;
And how you stooped as men whose strength was spent,
I knew that we had suffered each as other,
And could have grasped your hand and cried, "My brother!"

Joseph Lee

"—BUT A SHORT TIME TO LIVE"

Our little hour,—how swift it flies
    When poppies flare and lilies smile;
How soon the fleeting minute dies,
    Leaving us but a little while
To dream our dream, to sing our song,
    To pick the fruit, to pluck the flower,

The Gods—They do not give us long,—
  One little hour.

Our little hour,—how short it is
  When Love with dew-eyed loveliness
Raises her lips for ours to kiss
  And dies within our first caress.
Youth flickers out like wind-blown flame,
  Sweets of to-day to-morrow sour,
For Time and Death, relentless, claim
  Our little hour.

Our little hour,—how short a tune
  To wage our wars, to fan our hates,
To take our fill of armoured crime,
  To troop our banners, storm the gates.
Blood on the sword, our eyes blood-red,
  Blind in our puny reign of power,
Do we forget how soon is sped
  Our little hour?

Our little hour,—how soon it dies:
  How short a time to tell our beads,
To chant our feeble Litanies,
  To think sweet thoughts, to do good deeds.
The altar lights grow pale and dim,
  The bells hang silent in the tower—
So passes with the dying hymn
  Our little hour.

Leslie Coulson

BEFORE ACTION

By all the glories of the day,
And the cool evening's benison:
By the last sunset touch that lay
Upon the hills when day was done;
By beauty lavishly outpoured,

And blessings carelessly received,
By all the days that I have lived,
Make me a soldier, Lord.

By all of all men's hopes and fears,
And all the wonders poets sing,
The laughter of unclouded years,
And every sad and lovely thing:
By the romantic ages stored
With high endeavour that was his,
By all his mad catastrophes,
Make me a man, O Lord.

I, that on my familiar hill
Saw with uncomprehending eyes
A hundred of Thy sunsets spill
Their fresh and sanguine sacrifice,
Ere the sun swings his noonday sword
Must say good-bye to all of this:—
By all delights that I shall miss,
Help me to die, O Lord.

W. N. Hodgson ("Edward Melbourne")

COURAGE

Alone amid the battle-din untouched
    Stands out one figure beautiful, serene;
No grime of smoke nor reeking blood hath smutched
    The virgin brow of this unconquered queen.
She is the Joy of Courage vanquishing
    The unstilled tremors of the fearful heart;
And it is she that bids the poet sing,
    And gives to each the strength to bear his part.

Her eye shall not be dimmed, but as a flame
    Shall light the distant ages with its fire,
That men may know the glory of her name,
    That purified our souls of fear's desire.

And she doth calm our sorrow, soothe our pain,
   And she shall lead us back to peace again.

Dyneley Hussey

OPTIMISM

At last there'll dawn the last of the long year,
Of the long year that seemed to dream no end,
Whose every dawn but turned the world more drear,
And slew some hope, or led away some friend.
Or be you dark, or buffeting, or blind,
We care not, day, but leave not death behind.

The hours that feed on war go heavy-hearted,
Death is no fare wherewith to make hearts fain.
Oh, we are sick to find that they who started
With glamour in their eyes came not again.
O day, be long and heavy if you will,
But on our hopes set not a bitter heel.

For tiny hopes like tiny flowers of Spring
Will come, though death and ruin hold the land,
Though storms may roar they may not break the wing
Of the earthed lark whose song is ever bland.
Fell year unpitiful, slow days of scorn,
Your kind shall die, and sweeter days be born.

A. Victor Ratcliffe

THE BATTLEFIELD

Around no fire the soldiers sleep to-night,
   But lie a-wearied on the ice-bound field,
   With cloaks wrapt round their sleeping forms, to shield
Them from the northern winds. Ere comes the light
Of morn brave men must arm, stern foes to fight.
   The sentry stands, his limbs with cold congealed;

His head a-nod with sleep; he cannot yield,
Though sleep and snow in deadly force unite.

Amongst the sleepers lies the Boy awake,
And wide-eyed plans brave glories that transcend
The deeds of heroes dead; then dreams o'ertake
His tired-out brain, and lofty fancies blend
To one grand theme, and through all barriers break
To guard from hurt his faithful sleeping friend.

Sydney Oswald

"ON LES AURA!"

SOLDAT JACQUES BONHOMME LOQUITUR:

See you that stretch of shell-torn mud spotted with
pools of mire,
Crossed by a burst abandoned trench and tortured
strands of wire,
Where splintered pickets reel and sag and leprous
trench-rats play,
That scour the Devil's hunting-ground to seek their
carrion prey?
That is the field my father loved, the field that once
was mine,
The land I nursed for my child's child as my fathers
did long syne.

See there a mound of powdered stones, all flattened,
smashed, and torn,
Gone black with damp and green with slime?—Ere
you and I were born
My father's father built a house, a little house and
bare,
And there I brought my woman home—that heap of
rubble there!

The soil of France! Fat fields and green that bred my
blood and bone!
Each wound that scars my bosom's pride burns deeper
than my own.

But yet there is one thing to say—one thing that
pays for all,
Whatever lot our bodies know, whatever fate befall,
We hold the line! We hold it still! My fields are No
Man's Land,
But the good God is debonair and holds us by the
hand.
"On les aura!" See there! and there I soaked heaps
of huddled, grey!
My fields shall laugh—enriched by those who sought
them for a prey.

James H. Knight-Adkin

TO AN OLD LADY SEEN AT A GUESTHOUSE FOR SOLDIERS

Quiet thou didst stand at thine appointed place,
There was no press to purchase—younger grace
Attracts the youth of valour. Thou didst not know,
Like the old, kindly Martha, to and fro
To haste. Yet one could say, "In thine I prize
The strength of calm that held in Mary's eyes."
And when they came, thy gracious smile so wrought
They knew that they were given, not that they bought.
Thou didst not tempt to vauntings, and pretence
Was dumb before thy perfect woman's sense.
Blest who have seen, for they shall ever see
The radiance of thy benignity.

Alexander Robertson

THE CASUALTY CLEARING STATION

A bowl of daffodils,
A crimson-quilted bed,
Sheets and pillows white as snow—
White and gold and red—
And sisters moving to and fro,
With soft and silent tread.

So all my spirit fills
With pleasure infinite,
And all the feathered wings of rest
Seem flocking from the radiant West
To bear me thro' the night.

See, how they close me in.
They, and the sisters' arms.
One eye is closed, the other lid
Is watching how my spirit slid
Toward some red-roofed farms,
And having crept beneath them slept
Secure from war's alarms.

Gilbert Waterhouse

HILLS OF HOME

Oh! yon hills are filled with sunlight, and the green
leaves paled to gold,
And the smoking mists of Autumn hanging faintly
o'er the wold;
I dream of hills of other days whose sides I loved to
roam
When Spring was dancing through the lanes of those
distant hills of home.

The winds of heaven gathered there as pure and cold
as dew;

Wood-sorrel and wild violets along the hedgerows
grew,
The blossom on the pear-trees was as white as flakes
of foam
In the orchard 'neath the shadow of those distant
hills of home.

The first white frost in the meadow will be shining
there to-day
And the furrowed upland glinting warm beside the
woodland way;
There, a bright face and a clear hearth will be waiting
when I come,
And my heart is throbbing wildly for those distant
hills of home.

Malcolm Hemphrey

THE RED CROSS SPIRIT SPEAKS

Wherever war, with its red woes,
Or flood, or fire, or famine goes,
There, too, go I;
If earth in any quarter quakes
Or pestilence its ravage makes,
Thither I fly.

I kneel behind the soldier's trench,
I walk 'mid shambles' smear and stench,
The dead I mourn;
I bear the stretcher and I bend
O'er Fritz and Pierre and Jack to mend
What shells have torn.

I go wherever men may dare,
I go wherever woman's care
And love can live,
Wherever strength and skill can bring

Surcease to human suffering,
Or solace give.

I helped upon Haldora's shore;
With Hospitaller Knights I bore
The first red cross;
I was the Lady of the Lamp;
I saw in Solferino's camp
The crimson loss.

I am your pennies and your pounds;
I am your bodies on their rounds
Of pain afar:
I am *you*, doing what you would
If you were only where you could—
Your avatar.

The cross which on my arm I wear,
The flag which o'er my breast I bear,
Is but the sign
Of what you'd sacrifice for him
Who suffers on the hellish rim
Of war's red line.

John Finley

CHAPLAIN TO THE FORCES

["I have once more to remark upon the devotion to duty, courage, and contempt of danger which has characterized the work of the Chaplains of the Army throughout this campaign."—*Sir John French, in the Neuve Chapelle dispatch.*]

Ambassador of Christ you go
Up to the very gates of Hell,
Through fog of powder, storm of shell,
To speak your Master's message: "Lo,
The Prince of Peace is with you still,
His peace be with you, His good-will."

It is not small, your priesthood's price.
To be a man and yet stand by,
To hold your life while others die,
To bless, not share the sacrifice,
To watch the strife and take no part—
You with the fire at your heart.

But yours, for our great Captain Christ,
To know the sweat of agony,
The darkness of Gethsemane,
In anguish for these souls unpriced.
Vicegerent of God's pity you,
A sword must pierce your own soul through.

In the pale gleam of new-born day,
Apart in some tree-shadowed place,
Your altar but a packing-case,
Rude as the shed where Mary lay,
Your sanctuary the rain-drenched sod,
You bring the kneeling soldier God.

As sentinel you guard the gate
'Twixt life and death, and unto death
Speed the brave soul whose failing breath
Shudders not at the grip of Fate,
But answers, gallant to the end,
"Christ is the Word—and I his friend."

Then God go with you, priest of God,
For all is well and shall be well.
What though you tread the roads of Hell,
Your Captain these same ways has trod.
Above the anguish and the loss
Still floats the ensign of His Cross.

Winifred M. Letts

SONG OF THE RED CROSS

O gracious ones, we bless your name
  Upon our bended knee;
The voice of love with tongue of flame
  Records your charity.
Your hearts, your lives right willingly ye gave,
  That sacred ruth might shine;
Ye fell, bright spirits, brave amongst the brave,
  Compassionate, divine.

Example from your lustrous deeds
  The conqueror shall take,
Sowing sublime and fruitful seeds
  Of *aidos* in this ache.
And when our griefs have passed on gloomy wing,
  When friend and foe are sped,
Sons of a morning to be born shall sing
  The radiant Cross of Red;
Sons of a morning to be born shall sing
  The radiant Cross of Red.

Eden Phillpotts

THE HEALERS

In a vision of the night I saw them,
  In the battles of the night.
'Mid the roar and the reeling shadows of blood
  They were moving like light,

Light of the reason, guarded
  Tense within the will,
As a lantern under a tossing of boughs
  Burns steady and still.

With scrutiny calm, and with fingers
  Patient as swift

They bind up the hurts and the pain-writhen
    Bodies uplift,

Untired and defenceless; around them
    With shrieks in its breath
Bursts stark from the terrible horizon
    Impersonal death;

But they take not their courage from anger
    That blinds the hot being;
They take not their pity from weakness;
    Tender, yet seeing;

Feeling, yet nerved to the uttermost;
    Keen, like steel;
Yet the wounds of the mind they are stricken with,
    Who shall heal?

They endure to have eyes of the watcher
    In hell, and not swerve
For an hour from the faith that they follow,
    The light that they serve.

Man true to man, to his kindness
    That overflows all,
To his spirit erect in the thunder
    When all his forts fall,—

This light, in the tiger-mad welter,
    They serve and they save.
What song shall be worthy to sing of them—
    Braver than the brave?

Laurence Binyon

THE RED CROSS NURSES

Out where the line of battle cleaves
The horizon of woe
And sightless warriors clutch the leaves
The Red Cross nurses go.
In where the cots of agony
Mark death's unmeasured tide—
Bear up the battle's harvestry—
The Red Cross nurses glide.

Look! Where the hell of steel has torn
Its way through slumbering earth
The orphaned urchins kneel forlorn
And wonder at their birth.
Until, above them, calm and wise
With smile and guiding hand,
God looking through their gentle eyes,
The Red Cross nurses stand.

Thomas L. Masson

KILMENY

(A SONG OF THE TRAWLERS)

Dark, dark lay the drifters, against the red west,
As they shot their long meshes of steel overside;
And the oily green waters were rocking to rest
When *Kilmeny* went out, at the turn of the tide.
And nobody knew where that lassie would roam,
For the magic that called her was tapping unseen,
It was well nigh a week ere *Kilmeny* came home,
And nobody knew where *Kilmeny* had been.

She'd a gun at her bow that was Newcastle's best,
And a gun at her stern that was fresh from the Clyde,
And a secret her skipper had never confessed,
Not even at dawn, to his newly wed bride;

And a wireless that whispered above like a gnome,
The laughter of London, the boasts of Berlin.
O, it may have been mermaids that lured her from home,
But nobody knew where *Kilmeny* had been.

It was dark when *Kilmeny* came home from her quest,
With her bridge dabbled red where her skipper had died;
But she moved like a bride with a rose at her breast;
And "Well done, Kilmeny!" the admiral cried.

Now at sixty-four fathom a conger may come,
And nose at the bones of a drowned submarine;
But late in the evening *Kilmeny* came home,
And nobody knew where *Kilmeny* had been.

There's a wandering shadow that stares at the foam,
Though they sing all the night to old England, their queen,
Late, late in the evening *Kilmeny* came home,
And nobody knew where *Kilmeny* had been.

Alfred Noyes

THE MINE-SWEEPERS

Dawn off the Foreland—the young flood making
Jumbled and short and steep—
Black in the hollows and bright where it's breaking—
Awkward water to sweep.
"Mines reported in the fairway,
Warn all traffic and detain.
Sent up *Unity*, *Claribel*, *Assyrian*, *Stormcock*, and *Golden Gain*."

Noon off the Foreland—the first ebb making
Lumpy and strong in the bight.
Boom after boom, and the golf-hut shaking
And the jackdaws wild with fright.
"Mines located in the fairway,
Boats now working up the chain,
Sweepers—*Unity*, *Claribel*, *Assyrian*, *Stormcock*, and *Golden Gain*."

Dusk off the Foreland—the last light going
And the traffic crowding through,
And five damned trawlers with their syreens blowing
Heading the whole review!
"Sweep completed in the fairway.
No more mines remain.
Sent back *Unity*, *Claribel*, *Assyrian*, *Stormcock*, and *Golden Gain*."

Rudyard Kipling

MARE LIBERUM

You dare to say with perjured lips,
"We fight to make the ocean free"?
You, whose black trail of butchered ships
Bestrews the bed of every sea
Where German submarines have wrought
Their horrors! Have you never thought,—
What you call freedom, men call piracy!

Unnumbered ghosts that haunt the wave
Where you have murdered, cry you down;
And seamen whom you would not save,
Weave now in weed-grown depths a crown
Of shame for your imperious head,—
A dark memorial of the dead,—
Women and children whom you left to drown.

Nay, not till thieves are set to guard
The gold, and corsairs called to keep
O'er peaceful commerce watch and ward,
And wolves to herd the helpless sheep,
Shall men and women look to thee—
Thou ruthless Old Man of the Sea—
To safeguard law and freedom on the deep!

In nobler breeds we put our trust:
The nations in whose sacred lore
The "Ought" stands out above the "Must,"

And Honor rules in peace and war.
With these we hold in soul and heart,
With these we choose our lot and part,
Till Liberty is safe on sea and shore.

Henry van Dyke
February 11, 1917

THE DAWN PATROL

Sometimes I fly at dawn above the sea,
Where, underneath, the restless waters flow—
Silver, and cold, and slow,
Dim in the east there burns a new-born sun,
Whose rosy gleams along the ripples run,
Save where the mist droops low,
Hiding the level loneliness from me.

And now appears beneath the milk-white haze
A little fleet of anchored ships, which lie
In clustered company,
And seem as they are yet fast bound by sleep,
Although the day has long begun to peep,
With red-inflamèd eye,
Along the still, deserted ocean ways.

The fresh, cold wind of dawn blows on my face
As in the sun's raw heart I swiftly fly,
And watch the seas glide by.
Scarce human seem I, moving through the skies,
And far removed from warlike enterprise—
Like some great gull on high
Whose white and gleaming wings beat on through space.

Then do I feel with God quite, quite alone,
High in the virgin morn, so white and still,
And free from human ill:
My prayers transcend my feeble earth-bound plaints—
As though I sang among the happy Saints

With many a holy thrill—
As though the glowing sun were God's bright Throne.

My flight is done. I cross the line of foam
That breaks around a town of grey and red,
Whose streets and squares lie dead
Beneath the silent dawn—then am I proud
That England's peace to guard I am allowed;
Then bow my humble head,
In thanks to Him Who brings me safely home.

Paul Bewsher

DESTROYERS OFF JUTLAND

["If lost hounds could speak when they cast up next day after an unchecked night among the wild life of the dark they would talk much as our destroyers do."—*Rudyard Kipling.*]

They had hot scent across the spumy sea,
Gehenna and her sister, swift *Shaitan*,
That in the pack, with *Goblin*, *Eblis* ran
And many a couple more, full cry, foot-free;
The dog-fox and his brood were fain to flee,
But bare of fang and dangerous to the van
That pressed them close. So when the kill began
Some hounds were lamed and some died splendidly.

But from the dusk along the Skagerack,
Until dawn loomed upon the Reef of Horn
And the last fox had slunk back to his earth,
They kept the great traditions of the pack,
Staunch-hearted through the hunt, as they were born,
These hounds that England suckled at the birth.

Reginald McIntosh Cleveland

BRITISH MERCHANT SERVICE

Oh, down by Millwall Basin as I went the other day,
I met a skipper that I knew, and to him I did say:
"Now what's the cargo, Captain, that brings you up this way?"

"Oh, I've been up and down (said he) and round about also . . .
From Sydney to the Skagerack, and Kiel to Callao . . .
With a leaking steam-pipe all the way to Californ-i-o . . .

"With pots and pans and ivory fans and every kind of thing,
Rails and nails and cotton bales, and sewer pipes and string . . .
But now I'm through with cargoes, and I'm here to serve the King!

"And if it's sweeping mines (to which my fancy somewhat leans)
Or hanging out with booby-traps for the skulking submarines,
I'm here to do my blooming best and give the beggars beans!

"A rough job and a tough job is the best job for me,
And what or where I don't much care, I'll take what it may be,
For a tight place is the right place when it's foul weather at sea!"

* * * * *

There's not a port he doesn't know from Melbourne to New York;
He's as hard as a lump of harness beef, and as salt as pickled pork . . .
And he'll stand by a wreck in a murdering gale and count it part of
    his work!

He's the terror of the fo'c's'le when he heals its various ills
With turpentine and mustard leaves, and poultices and pills . . .
But he knows the sea like the palm of his hand, as a shepherd
    knows the hills.

He'll spin you yarns from dawn to dark—and half of 'em are
    true!
He swears in a score of languages, and maybe talks in two!
And . . . he'll lower a boat in a hurricane to save a drowning crew.

A rough job or a tough job—he's handled two or three—
And what or where he won't much care, nor ask what the risk may
be . . .
For a tight place is the right place when it's wild weather at sea!

C. Fox Smith

TO A SOLDIER IN HOSPITAL

Courage came to you with your boyhood's grace
Of ardent life and limb.
Each day new dangers steeled you to the test,
To ride, to climb, to swim.
Your hot blood taught you carelessness of death
With every breath.

So when you went to play another game
You could not but be brave:
An Empire's team, a rougher football field,
The end—perhaps your grave.
What matter? On the winning of a goal
You staked your soul.

Yes, you wore courage as you wore your youth
With carelessness and joy.
But in what Spartan school of discipline
Did you get patience, boy?
How did you learn to bear this long-drawn pain
And not complain?

Restless with throbbing hopes, with thwarted aims,
Impulsive as a colt,
How do you lie here month by weary month
Helpless, and not revolt?
What joy can these monotonous days afford
Here in a ward?

Yet you are merry as the birds in spring,
Or feign the gaiety,

Lest those who dress and tend your wound each day
Should guess the agony.
Lest they should suffer—this the only fear
You let draw near.

Greybeard philosophy has sought in books
And argument this truth,
That man is greater than his pain, but you
Have learnt it in your youth.
You know the wisdom taught by Calvary
At twenty-three.

Death would have found you brave, but braver still
You face each lagging day,
A merry Stoic, patient, chivalrous,
Divinely kind and gay.
You bear your knowledge lightly, graduate
Of unkind Fate.

Careless philosopher, the first to laugh,
The latest to complain.
Unmindful that you teach, you taught me this
In your long fight with pain:
Since God made man so good—here stands my creed—
God's good indeed.

Winifred M. Letts

BETWEEN THE LINES

When consciousness came back, he found he lay
Between the opposing fires, but could not tell
On which hand were his friends; and either way
For him to turn was chancy—bullet and shell
Whistling and shrieking over him, as the glare
Of searchlights scoured the darkness to blind day.
He scrambled to his hands and knees ascare,
Dragging his wounded foot through puddled clay,
And tumbled in a hole a shell had scooped

At random in a turnip-field between
The unseen trenches where the foes lay cooped
Through that unending-battle of unseen,
Dead-locked, league-stretching armies; and quite spent
He rolled upon his back within the pit,
And lay secure, thinking of all it meant—
His lying in that little hole, sore hit,
But living, while across the starry sky
Shrapnel and shell went screeching overhead—
Of all it meant that he, Tom Dodd, should lie
Among the Belgian turnips, while his bed . . .
If it were he, indeed, who'd climbed each night,
Fagged with the day's work, up the narrow stair,
And slipt his clothes off in the candle-light,
Too tired to fold them neatly in a chair
The way his mother'd taught him—too dog-tired
After the long day's serving in the shop,
Inquiring what each customer required,
Politely talking weather, fit to drop . . .

And now for fourteen days and nights, at least,
He hadn't had his clothes off, and had lain
In muddy trenches, napping like a beast
With one eye open, under sun and rain
And that unceasing hell-fire . . .
It was strange
How things turned out—the chances! You'd just got
To take your luck in life, you couldn't change
Your luck.
And so here he was lying shot
Who just six months ago had thought to spend
His days behind a counter. Still, perhaps . . .
And now, God only knew how he would end!

He'd like to know how many of the chaps
Had won back to the trench alive, when he
Had fallen wounded and been left for dead,
If any! . . .
This was different, certainly,

From selling knots of tape and reels of thread
And knots of tape and reels of thread and knots
Of tape and reels of thread and knots of tape,
Day in, day out, and answering "Have you got"'s
And "Do you keep"'s till there seemed no escape
From everlasting serving in a shop,
Inquiring what each customer required,
Politely talking weather, fit to drop,
With swollen ankles, tired . . .

But he was tired
Now. Every bone was aching, and had ached
For fourteen days and nights in that wet trench—
Just duller when he slept than when he waked—
Crouching for shelter from the steady drench
Of shell and shrapnel . . .

That old trench, it seemed
Almost like home to him. He'd slept and fed
And sung and smoked in it, while shrapnel screamed
And shells went whining harmless overhead—
Harmless, at least, as far as he . . .

But Dick—
Dick hadn't found them harmless yesterday,
At breakfast, when he'd said he couldn't stick
Eating dry bread, and crawled out the back way,
And brought them butter in a lordly dish—
Butter enough for all, and held it high,
Yellow and fresh and clean as you would wish—
When plump upon the plate from out the sky
A shell fell bursting . . . Where the butter went,
God only knew! . . .

And Dick . . . He dared not think
Of what had come to Dick . . . or what it meant—
The shrieking and the whistling and the stink
He'd lived in fourteen days and nights. 'T was luck
That he still lived . . . And queer how little then
He seemed to care that Dick . . . perhaps 't was pluck
That hardened him—a man among the men—
Perhaps . . . Yet, only think things out a bit,
And he was rabbit-livered, blue with funk!

And he'd liked Dick . . . and yet when Dick was hit
He hadn't turned a hair. The meanest skunk
He should have thought would feel it when his mate
Was blown to smithereens—Dick, proud as punch,
Grinning like sin, and holding up the plate—
But he had gone on munching his dry hunch,
Unwinking, till he swallowed the last crumb.
Perhaps 't was just because he dared not let
His mind run upon Dick, who'd been his chum.
He dared not now, though he could not forget.

Dick took his luck. And, life or death, 't was luck
From first to last; and you'd just got to trust
Your luck and grin. It wasn't so much pluck
As knowing that you'd got to, when needs must,
And better to die grinning . . .

Quiet now
Had fallen on the night. On either hand
The guns were quiet. Cool upon his brow
The quiet darkness brooded, as he scanned
The starry sky. He'd never seen before
So many stars. Although, of course, he'd known
That there were stars, somehow before the war
He'd never realised them—so thick-sown,
Millions and millions. Serving in the shop,
Stars didn't count for much; and then at nights
Strolling the pavements, dull and fit to drop,
You didn't see much but the city lights.
He'd never in his life seen so much sky
As he'd seen this last fortnight. It was queer
The things war taught you. He'd a mind to try
To count the stars—they shone so bright and clear.

One, two, three, four . . . Ah, God, but he was tired . . .
Five, six, seven, eight . . .

Yes, it was number eight.
And what was the next thing that she required?
(Too bad of customers to come so late,
At closing time!) Again within the shop

He handled knots of tape and reels of thread,
Politely talking weather, fit to drop . . .

When once again the whole sky overhead
Flared blind with searchlights, and the shriek of shell
And scream of shrapnel roused him. Drowsily
He stared about him, wondering. Then he fell
Into deep dreamless slumber.

* * * * *

He could see
Two dark eyes peeping at him, ere he knew
He was awake, and it again was day—
An August morning, burning to clear blue.
The frightened rabbit scuttled . . .
Far away,
A sound of firing . . . Up there, in the sky
Big dragon-flies hung hovering . . . Snowballs burst
About them . . . Flies and snowballs. With a cry
He crouched to watch the airmen pass—the first
That he'd seen under fire. Lord, that was pluck—
Shells bursting all about them—and what nerve!
They took their chance, and trusted to their luck.
At such a dizzy height to dip and swerve,
Dodging the shell-fire . . .
Hell! but one was hit,
And tumbling like a pigeon, plump . . .
Thank Heaven,
It righted, and then turned; and after it
The whole flock followed safe—four, five, six, seven,
Yes, they were all there safe. He hoped they'd win
Back to their lines in safety. They deserved,
Even if they were Germans . . . 'T was no sin
To wish them luck. Think how that beggar swerved
Just in the nick of time!
He, too, must try
To win back to the lines, though, likely as not,
He'd take the wrong turn: but he couldn't lie

Forever in that hungry hole and rot,
He'd got to take his luck, to take his chance
Of being sniped by foes or friends. He'd be
With any luck in Germany or France
Or Kingdom-come, next morning . . .
Drearily
The blazing day burnt over him, shot and shell
Whistling and whining ceaselessly. But light
Faded at last, and as the darkness fell
He rose, and crawled away into the night.

Wilfrid Wilson Gibson

THE WHITE COMRADE

(AFTER W.H. LEATHAM'S *The Comrade in White*)

Under our curtain of fire,
Over the clotted clods,
We charged, to be withered, to reel
And despairingly wheel
When the bugles bade us retire
From the terrible odds.

As we ebbed with the battle-tide,
Fingers of red-hot steel
Suddenly closed on my side.
I fell, and began to pray.
I crawled on my hands and lay
Where a shallow crater yawned wide;
Then,—I swooned . . .

When I woke, it was yet day.
Fierce was the pain of my wound,
But I saw it was death to stir,
For fifty paces away
Their trenches were.
In torture I prayed for the dark
And the stealthy step of my friend

Who, staunch to the very end,
Would creep to the danger zone
And offer his life as a mark
To save my own.

Night fell. I heard his tread,
Not stealthy, but firm and serene,
As if my comrade's head
Were lifted far from that scene
Of passion and pain and dread;
As if my comrade's heart
In carnage took no part;
As if my comrade's feet
Were set on some radiant street
Such as no darkness might haunt;
As if my comrade's eyes,
No deluge of flame could surprise,
No death and destruction daunt,
No red-beaked bird dismay,
Nor sight of decay.

Then in the bursting shells' dim light
I saw he was clad in white.
For a moment I thought that I saw the smock
Of a shepherd in search of his flock.
Alert were the enemy, too,
And their bullets flew
Straight at a mark no bullet could fail;
For the seeker was tall and his robe was bright;
But he did not flee nor quail.
Instead, with unhurrying stride
He came,
And gathering my tall frame,
Like a child, in his arms . . .

Again I swooned,
And awoke
From a blissful dream
In a cave by a stream.

My silent comrade had bound my side.
No pain now was mine, but a wish that I spoke,—
A mastering wish to serve this man
Who had ventured through hell my doom to revoke,
As only the truest of comrades can.
I begged him to tell me how best I might aid him,
And urgently prayed him
Never to leave me, whatever betide;
When I saw he was hurt—
Shot through the hands that were clasped in prayer!
Then, as the dark drops gathered there
And fell in the dirt,
The wounds of my friend
Seemed to me such as no man might bear.
Those bullet-holes in the patient hands
Seemed to transcend
All horrors that ever these war-drenched lands
Had known or would know till the mad world's end.
Then suddenly I was aware
That his feet had been wounded, too;
And, dimming the white of his side,
A dull stain grew.
"You are hurt, White Comrade!" I cried.
His words I already foreknew:
"These are old wounds," said he,
"But of late they have troubled me."

Robert Haven Schauffler

FLEURETTE

THE WOUNDED CANADIAN SPEAKS:

My leg? It's off at the knee.
Do I miss it? Well, some. You see
I've had it since I was born;
And lately a devilish corn.
(I rather chuckle with glee
To think how I've fooled that corn.)

But I'll hobble around all right.
It isn't that, it's my face.
Oh, I know I'm a hideous sight,
Hardly a thing in place.
Sort of gargoyle, you'd say.
Nurse won't give me a glass,
But I see the folks as they pass
Shudder and turn away;
Turn away in distress . . .
Mirror enough, I guess.
I'm gay! You bet I *am* gay,
But I wasn't a while ago.
If you'd seen me even to-day,
The darnedest picture of woe,
With this Caliban mug of mine,
So ravaged and raw and red,
Turned to the wall—in fine
Wishing that I was dead . . .
What has happened since then,
Since I lay with my face to the wall,
The most despairing of men!
Listen! I'll tell you all.

That *poilu* across the way,
With the shrapnel wound on his head,
Has a sister: she came to-day
To sit awhile by his bed.
All morning I heard him fret:
"Oh, when will she come, Fleurette?"

Then sudden, a joyous cry;
The tripping of little feet;
The softest, tenderest sigh;
A voice so fresh and sweet;
Clear as a silver bell,
Fresh as the morning dews:
"C'est toi, c'est toi, Marcel!
Mon frère, comme je suis heureuse!"

So over the blanket's rim
I raised my terrible face,
And I saw—how I envied him!
A girl of such delicate grace;
Sixteen, all laughter and love;
As gay as a linnet, and yet
As tenderly sweet as a dove;
Half woman, half child—Fleurette.

Then I turned to the wall again.
(I was awfully blue, you see,)
And I thought with a bitter pain:
"Such visions are not for me."
So there like a log I lay,
All hidden, I thought, from view,
When sudden I heard her say:
"Ah! Who is that *malheureux*?"
Then briefly I heard him tell
(However he came to know)
How I'd smothered a bomb that fell
Into the trench, and so
None of my men were hit,
Though it busted me up a bit.

Well, I didn't quiver an eye,
And he chattered and there she sat;
And I fancied I heard her sigh—
But I wouldn't just swear to that.
And maybe she wasn't so bright,
Though she talked in a merry strain,
And I closed my eyes ever so tight,
Yet I saw her ever so plain:
Her dear little tilted nose,
Her delicate, dimpled chin,
Her mouth like a budding rose,
And the glistening pearls within;
Her eyes like the violet:
Such a rare little queen—Fleurette.

And at last when she rose to go,
The light was a little dim,
And I ventured to peep, and so
I saw her, graceful and slim,
And she kissed him and kissed him, and oh
How I envied and envied him!

So when she was gone I said
In rather a dreary voice
To him of the opposite bed:
"Ah, friend, how you must rejoice!
But me, I'm a thing of dread.
For me nevermore the bliss,
The thrill of a woman's kiss."

Then I stopped, for lo! she was there,
And a great light shone in her eyes.
And me! I could only stare,
I was taken so by surprise,
When gently she bent her head:
"May I kiss you, sergeant?" she said.

Then she kissed my burning lips,
With her mouth like a scented flower,
And I thrilled to the finger-tips,
And I hadn't even the power
To say: "God bless you, dear!"
And I felt such a precious tear
Pall on my withered cheek,
And darn it! I couldn't speak.

And so she went sadly away,
And I know that my eyes were wet.
Ah, not to my dying day
Will I forget, forget!
Can you wonder now I am gay?
God bless her, that little Fleurette!

Robert W. Service

NOT TO KEEP

They sent him back to her. The letter came
Saying . . . and she could have him. And before
She could be sure there was no hidden ill
Under the formal writing, he was in her sight—
Living.—They gave him back to her alive—
How else? They are not known to send the dead—
And not disfigured visibly. His face?—
His hands? She had to look—to ask,
"What was it, dear?" And she had given all
And still she had all—*they* had—they the lucky!
Wasn't she glad now? Everything seemed won,
And all the rest for them permissible ease.
She had to ask, "What was it, dear?"

"Enough,
Yet not enough. A bullet through and through,
High in the breast. Nothing but what good care
And medicine and rest—and you a week,
Can cure me of to go again." The same
Grim giving to do over for them both.
She dared no more than ask him with her eyes
How was it with him for a second trial.
And with his eyes he asked her not to ask.
They had given him back to her, but not to keep.

Robert Frost

THE DEAD

I

Blow out, you bugles, over the rich Dead!
There's none of these so lonely and poor of old,
But, dying, has made us rarer gifts than gold.
These laid the world away; poured out the red
Sweet wine of youth; gave up the years to be
Of work and joy, and that unhoped serene,

That men call age; and those who would have been,
Their sons, they gave, their immortality.

Blow, bugles, blow! They brought us, for our dearth,
Holiness, lacked so long, and Love, and Pain.
Honour has come back, as a king, to earth,
And paid his subjects with a royal wage;
And Nobleness walks in our ways again;
And we have come into our heritage.

II

These hearts were woven of human joys and cares
Washed marvellously with sorrow, swift to mirth.
The years had given them kindness. Dawn was theirs,
And sunset, and the colours of the earth.
These had seen movement and heard music; known
Slumber and waking; loved; gone proudly friended;
Felt the quick stir of wonder; sat alone;
Touched flowers and furs and cheeks. All this is ended.
There are waters blown by changing winds to laughter
And lit by the rich skies, all day. And after,
Frost, with a gesture, stays the waves that dance
And wandering loveliness. He leaves a white
Unbroken glory, a gathered radiance,
A width, a shining peace, under the night.

Rupert Brooke

THE ISLAND OF SKYROS

Here, where we stood together, we three men,
Before the war had swept us to the East
Three thousand miles away, I stand again
And bear the bells, and breathe, and go to feast.
We trod the same path, to the selfsame place,
Yet here I stand, having beheld their graves,
Skyros whose shadows the great seas erase,
And Seddul Bahr that ever more blood craves.

So, since we communed here, our bones have been
Nearer, perhaps, than they again will be,
Earth and the worldwide battle lie between,
Death lies between, and friend-destroying sea.
Yet here, a year ago, we talked and stood
As I stand now, with pulses beating blood.

I saw her like a shadow on the sky
In the last light, a blur upon the sea,
Then the gale's darkness put the shadow by,
But from one grave that island talked to me;
And, in the midnight, in the breaking storm,
I saw its blackness and a blinking light,
And thought, "So death obscures your gentle form,
So memory strives to make the darkness bright;
And, in that heap of rocks, your body lies,
Part of the island till the planet ends,
My gentle comrade, beautiful and wise,
Part of this crag this bitter surge offends,
While I, who pass, a little obscure thing,
War with this force, and breathe, and am its king."

John Masefield

FOR THE FALLEN

With proud thanksgiving, a mother for her children,
England mourns for her dead across the sea.
Flesh of her flesh they were, spirit of her spirit,
Fallen in the cause of the free.

Solemn the drums thrill; Death august and royal
Sings sorrow up into immortal spheres,
There is music in the midst of desolation
And a glory that shines upon our tears.

They went with songs to the battle, they were young,
Straight of limb, true of eye, steady and aglow.

They were staunch to the end against odds uncounted:
They fell with their faces to the foe.

They shall grow not old, as we that are left grow old:
Age shall not weary them, nor the years condemn.
At the going down of the sun and in the morning
We will remember them.

They mingle not with their laughing comrades again;
They sit no more at familiar tables of home;
They have no lot in our labour of the day-time;
They sleep beyond England's foam.

But where our desires are and our hopes profound,
Felt as a well-spring that is hidden from sight,
To the innermost heart of their own land they are known
As the stars are known to the Night;

As the stars that shall be bright when we are dust,
Moving in marches upon the heavenly plain;
As the stars that are starry in the time of our darkness,
To the end, to the end, they remain.

Laurence Binyon

TWO SONNETS

I

Saints have adored the lofty soul of you.
Poets have whitened at your high renown.
We stand among the many millions who
Do hourly wait to pass your pathway down.
You, so familiar, once were strange: we tried
To live as of your presence unaware.
But now in every road on every side
We see your straight and steadfast signpost there.

I think it like that signpost in my land
Hoary and tall, which pointed me to go
Upward, into the hills, on the right hand,
Where the mists swim and the winds shriek and blow,
A homeless land and friendless, but a land
I did not know and that I wished to know.

II

Such, such is Death: no triumph: no defeat:
Only an empty pail, a slate rubbed clean,
A merciful putting away of what has been.

And this we know: Death is not Life effete,
Life crushed, the broken pail. We who have seen
So marvellous things know well the end not yet.

Victor and vanquished are a-one in death:
Coward and brave: friend, foe. Ghosts do not say,
"Come, what was your record when you drew breath?"
But a big blot has hid each yesterday
So poor, so manifestly incomplete.
And your bright Promise, withered long and sped,
Is touched, stirs, rises, opens and grows sweet
And blossoms and is you, when you are dead.

Charles Hamilton Sorley
June 12, 1915

"HOW SLEEP THE BRAVE"

Nay, nay, sweet England, do not grieve!
Not one of these poor men who died
But did within his soul believe
That death for thee was glorified.

Ever they watched it hovering near
That mystery 'yond thought to plumb,

Perchance sometimes in loathed fear
    They heard cold Danger whisper, Come!—

Heard and obeyed. O, if thou weep
    Such courage and honour, beauty, care,
Be it for joy that those who sleep
    Only thy joy could share.

Walter de la Mare

THE DEBT

No more old England will they see—
Those men who've died for you and me.

So lone and cold they lie; but we,
We still have life; we still may greet
Our pleasant friends in home and street;
We still have life, are able still
To climb the turf of Bignor Hill,
To see the placid sheep go by,
To hear the sheep-dog's eager cry,
To feel the sun, to taste the rain,
To smell the Autumn's scents again
Beneath the brown and gold and red
Which old October's brush has spread,
To hear the robin in the lane,
To look upon the English sky.

So young they were, so strong and well,
Until the bitter summons fell—
Too young to die.
Yet there on foreign soil they lie,
So pitiful, with glassy eye
And limbs all tumbled anyhow:
Quite finished, now.
On every heart—lest we forget—
Secure at home—engrave this debt!

Too delicate is flesh to be
The shield that nations interpose
'Twixt red Ambition and his foes—
The bastion of Liberty.
So beautiful their bodies were,
Built with so exquisite a care:
So young and fit and lithe and fair.
The very flower of us were they,
The very flower, but yesterday!
Yet now so pitiful they lie,
Where love of country bade them hie
To fight this fierce Caprice—and die.
All mangled now, where shells have burst,
And lead and steel have done their worst;
The tender tissues ploughed away,
The years' slow processes effaced:
The Mother of us all—disgraced.

And some leave wives behind, young wives;
Already some have launched new lives:
A little daughter, little son—
For thus this blundering world goes on.
But never more will any see
The old secure felicity,
The kindnesses that made us glad
Before the world went mad.
They'll never hear another bird,
Another gay or loving word—
Those men who lie so cold and lone,
Far in a country not their own;
Those men who died for you and me,
That England still might sheltered be
And all our lives go on the same
(Although to live is almost shame).

E.V. Lucas

REQUIESCANT

In lonely watches night by night
Great visions burst upon my sight,
For down the stretches of the sky
The hosts of dead go marching by.

Strange ghostly banners o'er them float,
Strange bugles sound an awful note,
And all their faces and their eyes
Are lit with starlight from the skies.

The anguish and the pain have passed
And peace hath come to them at last,
But in the stern looks linger still
The iron purpose and the will.

Dear Christ, who reign'st above the flood
Of human tears and human blood,
A weary road these men have trod,
O house them in the home of God!

Frederick George Scott
In a Field near Ypres
April, 1915

TO OUR FALLEN

Ye sleepers, who will sing you?
    We can but give our tears—
Ye dead men, who shall bring you
    Fame in the coming years?
Brave souls . . . but who remembers
The flame that fired your embers? . . .
Deep, deep the sleep that holds you
    Who one time had no peers.

Yet maybe Fame's but seeming
    And praise you'd set aside,

Content to go on dreaming,
    Yea, happy to have died
If of all things you prayed for—
All things your valour paid for—
One prayer is not forgotten,
    One purchase not denied.

But God grants your dear England
    A strength that shall not cease
Till she have won for all the Earth
    From ruthless men release,
And made supreme upon her
Mercy and Truth and Honour—
Is this the thing you died for?
    Oh, Brothers, sleep in peace!

Robert Ernest Vernède

THE OLD SOLDIER

Lest the young soldiers be strange in heaven,
    God bids the old soldier they all adored
Come to Him and wait for them, clean, new-shriven,
    A happy doorkeeper in the House of the Lord.

Lest it abash them, the strange new splendour,
    Lest it affright them, the new robes clean;
Here's an old face, now, long-tried, and tender,
    A word and a hand-clasp as they troop in.

"My boys," he greets them: and heaven is homely,
    He their great captain in days gone o'er;
Dear is the friend's face, honest and comely,
    Waiting to welcome them by the strange door.

Katharine Tynan

LORD KITCHENER

Unflinching hero, watchful to foresee
  And face thy country's peril wheresoe'er,
  Directing war and peace with equal care,
Till by long duty ennobled thou wert he
Whom England call'd and bade "Set my arm free
  To obey my will and save my honour fair,"—
  What day the foe presumed on her despair
And she herself had trust in none but thee:

Among Herculean deeds the miracle
  That mass'd the labour of ten years in one
  Shall be thy monument. Thy work was done
Ere we could thank thee; and the high sea swell
Surgeth unheeding where thy proud ship fell
  By the lone Orkneys, at the set of sun.

Robert Bridges
June 8, 1916

KITCHENER

There is wild water from the north;
The headlands darken in their foam
As with a threat of challenge stubborn earth
Booms at that far wild sea-line charging home.

The night shall stand upon the shifting sea
As yesternight stood there,
And hear the cry of waters through the air,
The iron voice of headlands start and rise—
The noise of winds for mastery
That screams to hear the thunder in those cries.
But now henceforth there shall be heard
From Brough of Bursay, Marwick Head,
And shadows of the distant coast,
Another voice bestirred—
Telling of something greatly lost

Somewhere below the tidal glooms, and dead.
Beyond the uttermost
Of aught the night may hear on any seas
From tempest-known wild water's cry, and roar
Of iron shadows looming from the shore,
It shall be heard—and when the Orcades
Sleep in a hushed Atlantic's starry folds
As smoothly as, far down below the tides,
Sleep on the windless broad sea-wolds
Where this night's shipwreck hides.

By many a sea-holm where the shock
Of ocean's battle falls, and into spray
Gives up its ghosts of strife; by reef and rock
Ravaged by their eternal brute affray
With monstrous frenzies of their shore's green foe;
Where overstream and overfall and undertow
Strive, snatch away;
A wistful voice, without a sound,
Shall dwell beside Pomona, on the sea,
And speak the homeward-and the outward-bound,
And touch the helm of passing minds
And bid them steer as wistfully—
Saying: "He did great work, until the winds
And waters hereabout that night betrayed
Him to the drifting death! His work went on—
He would not be gainsaid . . .
Though where his bones are, no man knows, not one!"

John Helston

THE FALLEN SUBALTERN

The starshells float above, the bayonets glisten;
  We bear our fallen friend without a sound;
Below the waiting legions lie and listen
  To us, who march upon their burial-ground.

Wound in the flag of England, here we lay him;
The guns will flash and thunder o'er the grave;
What other winding sheet should now array him,
What other music should salute the brave?

As goes the Sun-god in his chariot glorious,
When all his golden banners are unfurled,
So goes the soldier, fallen but victorious,
And leaves behind a twilight in the world.

And those who come this way, in days hereafter,
Will know that here a boy for England fell,
Who looked at danger with the eyes of laughter,
And on the charge his days were ended well.

One last salute; the bayonets clash and glisten;
With arms reversed we go without a sound:
One more has joined the men who lie and listen
To us, who march upon their burial-ground.

Herbert Asquith
1915

THE DEBT UNPAYABLE

What have I given,
Bold sailor on the sea,
In earth or heaven,
That you should die for me?

What can I give,
O soldier, leal and brave,
Long as I live,
To pay the life you gave?

What tithe or part
Can I return to thee,
O stricken heart,
That thou shouldst break for me?

The wind of Death
    For you has slain life's flowers,
It withereth
    (God grant) all weeds in ours.

F.W. Bourdillon

THE MESSAGES

"I cannot quite remember . . . There were five
Dropt dead beside me in the trench—and three
Whispered their dying messages to me . . ."

Back from the trenches, more dead than alive,
Stone-deaf and dazed, and with a broken knee,
He hobbled slowly, muttering vacantly:

"I cannot quite remember . . . There were five
Dropt dead beside me in the trench, and three
Whispered their dying messages to me . . .

"Their friends are waiting, wondering how they thrive—
Waiting a word in silence patiently . . .
But what they said, or who their friends may be

"I cannot quite remember . . . There were five
Dropt dead beside me in the trench—and three
Whispered their dying messages to me . . ."

Wilfrid Wilson Gibson

A CROSS IN FLANDERS

In the face of death, they say, he joked—he had no fear;
    His comrades, when they laid him in a Flanders grave,
Wrote on a rough-hewn cross—a Calvary stood near—
    "Without a fear he gave

"His life, cheering his men, with laughter on his lips."
So wrote they, mourning him. Yet was there only one
Who fully understood his laughter, his gay quips,
One only, she alone—

She who, not so long since, when love was new—confest,
Herself toyed with light laughter while her eyes were dim,
And jested, while with reverence despite her jest
She worshipped God and him.

She knew—O Love, O Death!—his soul had been at grips
With the most solemn things. For *she*, was *she* not dear?
Yes, he was brave, most brave, with laughter on his lips,
The braver for his fear!

G. Rostrevor Hamilton

RESURRECTION

Not long did we lie on the torn, red field of pain.
We fell, we lay, we slumbered, we took rest,
With the wild nerves quiet at last, and the vexed brain
Cleared of the wingèd nightmares, and the breast
Freed of the heavy dreams of hearts afar.
We rose at last under the morning star.
We rose, and greeted our brothers, and welcomed our foes.
We rose; like the wheat when the wind is over, we rose.
With shouts we rose, with gasps and incredulous cries,
With bursts of singing, and silence, and awestruck eyes,
With broken laughter, half tears, we rose from the sod,
With welling tears and with glad lips, whispering, "God."
Like babes, refreshed from sleep, like children, we rose,
Brimming with deep content, from our dreamless repose.
And, "What do you call it?" asked one. "I thought I was dead."
"You are," cried another. "We're all of us dead and flat."
"I'm alive as a cricket. There's something wrong with your head."

They stretched their limbs and argued it out where they sat.
And over the wide field friend and foe
Spoke of small things, remembering not old woe
Of war and hunger, hatred and fierce words.
They sat and listened to the brooks and birds,
And watched the starlight perish in pale flame,
Wondering what God would look like when He came.

Hermann Hagedorn

TO A HERO

We may not know how fared your soul before
  Occasion came to try it by this test.
Perchance, it used on lofty wings to soar;
  Again, it may have dwelt in lowly nest.

We do not know if bygone knightly strain
  Impelled you then, or blood of humble clod
Defied the dread adventure to attain
  The cross of honor or the peace of God.

We see but this, that when the moment came
  You raised on high, then drained, the solemn cup—
The grail of death; that, touched by valor's flame,
  The kindled spirit burned the body up.

Oscar C.A. Child

RUPERT BROOKE

(IN MEMORIAM)

I never knew you save as all men know
  Twitter of mating birds, flutter of wings
In April coverts, and the streams that flow—
  One of the happy voices of our Springs.

A voice for ever stilled, a memory,
Since you went eastward with the fighting ships,
A hero of the great new Odyssey,
And God has laid His finger on your lips.

Moray Dalton

THE PLAYERS

We challenged Death. He threw with weighted dice.
We laughed and paid the forfeit, glad to pay—
Being recompensed beyond our sacrifice
With that nor Death nor Time can take away.

Francis Bickley

A SONG

Oh, red is the English rose,
And the lilies of France are pale,
And the poppies grow in the golden wheat,
For the men whose eyes are heavy with sleep,
Where the ground is red as the English rose,
And the lips as the lilies of France are pale,
And the ebbing pulses beat fainter and fainter and fail.

Oh, red is the English rose,
And the lilies of France are pale.
And the poppies lie in the level corn
For the men who sleep and never return.
But wherever they lie an English rose
So red, and a lily of France so pale,
Will grow for a love that never and never can fail.

Charles Alexander Richmond

HARVEST MOON

Over the twilight field,
Over the glimmering field
And bleeding furrows, with their sodden yield
Of sheaves that still did writhe,
After the scythe;
The teeming field, and darkly overstrewn
With all the garnered fullness of that noon—
Two looked upon each other.
One was a Woman, men had called their mother:
And one the Harvest Moon.

And one the Harvest Moon
Who stood, who gazed
On those unquiet gleanings, where they bled;
Till the lone Woman said:

"But we were crazed . . .
We should laugh now together, I and you;
We two.
You, for your ever dreaming it was worth
A star's while to look on, and light the earth;
And I, for ever telling to my mind
Glory it was and gladness, to give birth
To human kind.
I gave the breath,—and thought it not amiss,
I gave the breath to men,
For men to slay again;
Lording it over anguish, all to give
My life, that men might live,
For this.

"You will be laughing now, remembering
We called you once Dead World, and barren thing.
Yes, so we called you then,
You, far more wise
Than to give life to men."

Over the field that there
Gave back the skies
A scattered upward stare
From sightless eyes,
The furrowed field that lay
Striving awhile, through many a bleeding dune
Of throbbing clay,—but dumb and quiet soon,
She looked; and went her way,
The Harvest Moon.

Josephine Preston Peabody

HARVEST MOON: 1916

Moon, slow rising, over the trembling sea-rim,
Moon of the lifted tides and their folded burden.
Look, look down. And gather the blinded oceans,
    Moon of compassion.

Come, white Silence, over the one sea pathway:
Pour with hallowing hands on the surge and outcry,
Silver flame; and over the famished blackness,
    Petals of moonlight.

Once again, the formless void of a world-wreck
Gropes its way through the echoing dark of chaos;
Tide on tide, to the calling, lost horizons,—
    One in the darkness.

You that veil the light of the all-beholding,
Shed white tidings down to the dooms of longing,
Down to the timeless dark; and the sunken treasures,
    One in the darkness.

Touch, and harken,—under that shrouding silver,
Rise and fall, the heart of the sea and its legions,
All and one; one with the breath of the deathless,
    Rising and falling.

Touch and waken so, to a far hereafter,
Ebb and flow, the deep, and the dead in their longing:
Till at last, on the hungering face of the waters,
        There shall be Light.

Light of Light, give us to see, for their sake.
Light of Light, grant them eternal peace;
And let light perpetual shine upon them;
                Light, everlasting.

Josephine Preston Peabody

MY SON

Here is his little cambric frock
        That I laid by in lavender so sweet,
And here his tiny shoe and sock
        I made with loving care for his dear feet.

I fold the frock across my breast,
        And in imagination, ah, my sweet,
Once more I hush my babe to rest,
        And once again I warm those little feet.

Where do those strong young feet now stand?
        In flooded trench, half numb to cold or pain,
Or marching through the desert sand
        To some dread place that they may never gain.

God guide him and his men to-day!
        Though death may lurk in any tree or hill,
His brave young spirit is their stay,
        Trusting in that they'll follow where he will.

They love him for his tender heart
        When poverty or sorrow asks his aid,
But he must see each do his part—
        Of cowardice alone he is afraid.

I ask no honours on the field,
        That other men have won as brave as he—
I only pray that God may shield
        My son, and bring him safely back to me!

Ada Tyrrell

TO THE OTHERS

This was the gleam then that lured from far
Your son and my son to the Holy War:
Your son and my son for the accolade
With the banner of Christ over them, in steel arrayed.

All quiet roads of life ran on to this;
When they were little for their mother's kiss.
Little feet hastening, so soft, unworn,
To the vows and the vigil and the road of thorn.

Your son and my son, the downy things,
Sheltered in mother's breast, by mother's wings,
Should they be broken in the Lord's wars—Peace!
He Who has given them—are they not His?

Dream of knight's armour and the battle-shout,
Fighting and falling at the last redoubt,
Dream of long dying on the field of slain;
This was the dream that lured, nor lured in vain.

These were the Voices they heard from far;
Bugles and trumpets of the Holy War.
Your son and my son have heard the call,
Your son and my son have stormed the wall.

Your son and my son, clean as new swords;
Your man and my man and now the Lord's!

Your son and my son for the Great Crusade,
With the banner of Christ over them—our knights new-made.

Katharine Tynan

THE JOURNEY

I went upon a journey
To countries far away,
From province unto province
To pass my holiday.

And when I came to Serbia,
In a quiet little town
At an inn with a flower-filled garden
With a soldier I sat down.

Now he lies dead at Belgrade.
You heard the cannon roar!
It boomed from Rome to Stockholm,
It pealed to the far west shore.

And when I came to Russia,
A man with flowing hair
Called me his friend and showed me
A flowing river there.

Now he lies dead at Lemberg,
Beside another stream,
In his dark eyes extinguished
The friendship of his dream.

And then I crossed two countries
Whose names on my lips are sealed . . .
Not yet had they flung their challenge
Nor led upon the field

Sons who lie dead at Liège,
Dead by the Russian lance,
Dead in southern mountains,
Dead through the farms of France.

I stopped in the land of Louvain,
So tranquil, happy, then.
I lived with a good old woman,
With her sons and her grandchildren.

Now they lie dead at Louvain,
Those simple kindly folk.
Some heard, some fled. It must be
Some slept, for they never woke.

I came to France. I was thirsty.
I sat me down to dine.
The host and his young wife served me
With bread and fruit and wine.

Now he lies dead at Cambrai—
He was sent among the first.
In dreams she sees him dying
Of wounds, of heat, of thirst.

At last I passed to Dover
And saw upon the shore
A tall young English captain
And soldiers, many more.

Now they lie dead at Dixmude,
The brave, the strong, the young!
I turn unto my homeland,
All my journey sung!

Grace Fallow Norton

A MOTHER'S DEDICATION

Dear son of mine, the baby days are over,
I can no longer shield you from the earth;
Yet in my heart always I must remember
How through the dark I fought to give you birth.

Dear son of mine, by all the lives behind you;
By all our fathers fought for in the past;
In this great war to which your birth has brought you,
Acquit you well, hold you our honour fast!

God guard you, son of mine, where'er you wander;
God lead the banners under which you fight;
You are my all, I give you to the Nation,
God shall uphold you that you fight aright.

Margaret Peterson

TO A MOTHER

Robbed mother of the stricken Motherland—
    Two hearts in one and one among the dead,
    Before your grave with an uncovered head
I, that am man, disquiet and silent stand
In reverence. It is your blood they shed;
    It is your sacred self that they demand,
    For one you bore in joy and hope, and planned
Would make yourself eternal, now has fled.

But though you yielded him unto the knife
    And altar with a royal sacrifice
Of your most precious self and dearer life—
    Your master gem and pearl above all price—
Content you; for the dawn this night restores
Shall be the dayspring of his soul and yours.

Eden Phillpotts

SPRING IN WAR-TIME

I feel the spring far off, far off,
    The faint, far scent of bud and leaf—
Oh, how can spring take heart to come
    To a world in grief,
    Deep grief?

The sun turns north, the days grow long,
    Later the evening star grows bright—
How can the daylight linger on
    For men to fight,
    Still fight?

The grass is waking in the ground,
    Soon it will rise and blow in waves—
How can it have the heart to sway
    Over the graves,
    New graves?

Under the boughs where lovers walked
    The apple-blooms will shed their breath—
But what of all the lovers now
    Parted by Death,
    Grey Death?

Sara Teasdale

OCCASIONAL NOTES

ASQUITH, HERBERT. He received a commission in the Royal Marine Artillery at the end of 1914 and served as a Second Lieutenant with an Anti-Aircraft Battery in April, 1915, returning wounded during the following June. He became a full Lieutenant in July, but was invalided home after about six weeks. In June, 1916, he joined the Royal Field Artillery and went out to France once again with a battery of field guns at the beginning of March, 1917. Since that time he has been steadily on active service.

BEWSHER, PAUL. He was educated at St. Paul's School, and is a Sub-Lieutenant in the Royal Naval Air Service.

BINYON, LAURENCE. His war writings include *The Winnowing Fan* and *The Anvil*, published in America under the title of *The Cause.*

BRIDGES, ROBERT. He has been Poet-Laureate of England since 1913.

BROOKE, RUPERT. He was born at Rugby on August 3, 1887, and became a Fellow of King's College, Cambridge, in 1913. He was made a Sub-Lieutenant in the Royal Naval Volunteer Reserve in September, 1914; accompanied the Antwerp expedition in October of the same year; and sailed with the British Mediterranean Expeditionary Force on February 28, 1915. He died in the Aegean, on April 23, and lies buried in the island of Skyros. See the memorial poems in this volume, *The Island of Skyros*, by John Masefield; and *Rupert Brooke*, by Moray Dalton. His war poetry appears in the volume entitled *1914 and other Poems*, and in his *Collected Poems.*

CAMPBELL, WILFRED. This well-known Canadian poet has lately published *Sagas of Vaster Britain, War Lyrics*, and *Canada's Responsibility to the Empire.* His son, Captain Basil Campbell, joined the Second Pioneers.

CHESTERTON, CECIL EDWARD. He has been editor of the *New Witness* since 1912, and is a private in the Highland Light Infantry. His war writings include *The Prussian hath said in his Heart*, and *The Perils of Peace.*

CHESTERTON, GILBERT KEITH. This brilliant and versatile author has written many essays on phases of the war, including weekly contributions to *The Illustrated London News.*

CONE, HELEN GRAY. She has been Professor of English in Hunter College since 1899. Her war poetry appears in the volume entitled *A Chant of Love for England, and other Poems.*

COULSON, LESLIE. He joined the British Army in September, 1914, declined a commission and served in Egypt, Malta, Gallipoli (where he was wounded), and Prance. He became Sergeant in the City of London Regiment (Royal Fusiliers) and was mortally wounded while leading a charge against the Germans in October, 1916.

DIXON, WILLIAM MACNEILE. He is Professor of English Language and Literature in the University of Glasgow. His war writings include *The British Navy at War* and *The Fleets behind the Fleet.*

DOYLE, SIR ARTHUR CONAN. He has written much of interest on the war, especially as regards the western campaigns.

FIELD, A.N. He is a private in the Second New Zealand Brigade.

FRANKAU, GILBERT. Upon the declaration of war he joined the Ninth East Surrey Regiment (Infantry), with the rank of Lieutenant. He was transferred to the Royal Field Artillery in March, 1915, and was appointed Adjutant during the following July. He proceeded to France in that capacity, fought in the battle of Loos, served at Ypres during the winter of 1915-16, and thereafter took part in the battle of the Somme. In

October, 1916, he was recalled to England, was promoted to the rank of Staff Captain in the Intelligence Corps, and was sent to Italy to engage in special duties.

FREEMAN, JOHN. He was Lieutenant-Colonel in the Russian A. M. S., on the Bacteriological Mission to Galicia, 1914.

GALSWORTHY, JOHN. Mr. Galsworthy, the well-known novelist, poet, and dramatist, served for several months as an expert *masseur* in an English hospital for French soldiers at Martouret.

GIBSON, WILFRID WILSON. His war writings include *Battle*, etc.

GRENFELL, THE HON. JULIAN, D.S.O. He was a Captain in the First Royal Dragoons; was wounded near Ypres on March 13, 1915; and died at Boulogne on May 26. He was the eldest son of Lord Desborough. "Julian set an example of light-hearted courage," wrote Lieutenant-Colonel Machlachan, of the Eighth Service Battalion Rifle Brigade, "which is famous all through the Army in France, and has stood out even above the most lion-hearted."

HALL, JAMES NORMAN. He is a member of the American Aviation Corps in France, and author of *Kitchener's Mob* and *High Adventure*. He was captured by the Germans, May 7, 1918, after an air battle inside the enemy's lines.

HARDY, THOMAS. He received the Order of Merit in 1910.

HEMPHREY, MALCOLM. He is a Lance-Corporal in the Army Ordnance Corps, Nairobi, British East Africa.

HEWLETT, MAURICE HENRY. He has published a group of his war poems under the title *Sing-Songs of the War*.

HODGSON, W.N. He was the son of the Bishop of Ipswich and Edmundsbury, and was a Lieutenant in the Devon Regiment. His pen-name is "Edward Melbourne." He won the Military Cross. He was killed during the battle of the Somme, in July, 1916.

HOWARD, GEOFFREY. He is a Lieutenant in the Royal Fusiliers.

HUSSEY, DYNELEY. He is a Lieutenant in the Thirteenth Battalion of the Lancashire Fusiliers, and has published his war poems in a volume entitled *Fleur de Lys.*

HUTCHINSON, HENRY WILLIAM. He was the son of Sir Sidney Hutchinson, and was educated at St. Paul's School. He was a Second Lieutenant in the Middlesex Regiment. He was killed while on active service in France, March 13, 1917, at the age of nineteen.

KAUFMAN, HERBERT. He has published *The Song of the Guns,* which was later republished as *The Hell-Gate of Soissons.*

KIPLING, RUDYARD. Mr. Kipling won the Nobel Prize for Literature in 1907. His war writings include *The New Armies in Training, France at War,* and *Sea Warfare.*

KNIGHT-ADKIN, JAMES. When war was declared he was a Master at the Imperial Service College, Windsor, and Lieutenant in the Officers' Training Corps. He volunteered on the first day of the war and was attached to the Fourth Battalion, Gloucester Regiment. He went into the trenches in March, 1915, was wounded in June, and was invalided home. In 1916 he returned to France, and is now a Captain in charge of a prisoner-of-war camp.

LEE, JOSEPH. He enlisted, at the outbreak of the war, as a private in the 1st/4th Battalion of the Black Watch, Royal Highlanders, in which corps he has served on all parts of the British front in France and Flanders. Sergeant Lee has both composed and illustrated a volume of war-poems entitled *Ballads of Battle.*

LUCAS, EDWARD VERRALL. Mr. Lucas has undertaken hospital service.

MASEFIELD, JOHN. Mr. Masefield, whose lectures in America early in 1916 quickened interest in his work and personality, has been very active during the war. He has written an excellent study of the campaign on the Gallipoli Peninsula, having served there and also in France in connection with Red Cross work.

MORGAN, CHARLES LANGBRIDGE. He is a Sub-Lieutenant in the Royal Naval Division, and is a Prisoner of War in Holland.

NEWBOLT, SIR HENRY. He is the author of *The Book of the Thin Red Line, Story of the Oxfordshire and Buckinghamshire Light Infantry*, and *Stories of the Great War.*

NOYES, ALFRED. His war writings include *A Salute to the Fleet*, etc.

OGILVIE, WILLIAM HENRY. He was Professor of Agricultural Journalism in the Iowa State College, U.S.A., from 1905 to 1907. His war writings include *Australia and Other Verses.*

OSWALD, SYDNEY. He is a Major in the King's Royal Rifle Corps.

PHILLIPS, STEPHEN. His war writings include *Armageddon*, etc. He died December 9, 1915.

PHILLPOTTS, EDEN. Among his war writings are *The Human Boy and the War*, and *Plain Song, 1914-16.*

RATCLIFFE, A. VICTOR. He was a Lieutenant in the 10th/13th West Yorkshire Regiment, and was killed in action on July 1, 1916.

RAWNSLEY, REV. HARDWICKE DRUMMOND. He has been Canon of Carlisle and Honorary Chaplain to the King since 1912.

ROBERTSON, ALEXANDER. He is a Corporal in the Twelfth York and Lancaster Regiment. He was reported "missing" in July, 1916.

ROSS, SIR RONALD. He is the President of the Poetry Society of Great Britain, and is a Lieutenant-Colonel in the Royal Army Medical Corps.

SCOLLARD, CLINTON. His war writings include *The Vale of Shadows, and Other Verses of the Great War*, and *Italy in Arms, and Other Verses.*

SCOTT, CANON FREDERICK GEORGE. He is a Major in the Third Brigade of the First Canadian Division, British Expeditionary Force.

SEAMAN, SIR OWEN. He has been the editor of *Punch* since 1906. His war writings include *War-Time* and *Made in England.*

SEEGER, ALAN. Among the Americans who have served at the front there is none who has produced poetic work of such high quality as that of Alan Seeger. He was born in New York on June 22nd, 1888; was educated at the Horace Mann School; Hackley School, Tarrytown, New York; and Harvard College. In 1912 he went to Paris and lived the life of a student and writer in the Latin Quarter. During the third week of the war he enlisted in the Foreign Legion of France. His service as a soldier was steady, loyal and uncomplaining—indeed, exultant would not be too strong a word to describe the spirit which seems constantly to have animated his military career. He took part in the battle of Champagne. Afterwards, his regiment was allowed to recuperate until May, 1916. On July 1 a general advance was ordered, and on the evening of July 4 the Legion was ordered to attack the village of Belloy-en-Santerre. Seeger's squad was caught by the fire of six machine-guns and he himself was wounded in several places, but he continued to cheer his comrades as they rushed on in what proved a successful charge. He died on the morning of July 5. The twenty or more poems he wrote during active service are included in the collected *Poems by Alan Seeger*, with an introduction by William Archer.

SORLEY, CHARLES HAMILTON. He was born at Old Aberdeen on May 19, 1895. He was a student at Marlborough College from the autumn of 1908 until the end of 1913, at which time he was elected to a scholarship at University College, Oxford. After leaving school in England, he spent several months as a student and observer in Germany. When the war broke out he returned home and was gazetted Second Lieutenant in the Seventh (Service) Battalion of the Suffolk Regiment. In November he was made a Lieutenant, and in August, 1915, a Captain. He served in France from May 30 to October 13, 1915, when he was killed in action near Hulluch. His war poems and letters appear in a volume entitled *Marlborough and other Poems*, published by the Cambridge University Press.

STEWART, J.E. He is a Captain in the Eighth Border Regiment, British Expeditionary Force. He was awarded the Military Cross in 1916.

TENNANT, EDWARD WYNDHAM. He was the son of Baron Glenconner, and was at Winchester when war was declared. He was only seventeen when he joined the Grenadier Guards, Twenty-first Battalion. He had one year's training in England, saw one year's active service in France, and fell, gallantly fighting, in the battle of the Somme, 1916.

TYNAN, KATHARINE. Pen-name of Mrs. Katharine Tynan Hinkson, whose war writings include *The Flower of Peace*, *The Holy War*, etc.

VAN DYKE, HENRY. He has been Professor of English Literature in Princeton University since 1900, and was United States Minister to the Netherlands and Luxembourg from June, 1913, to December, 1916. He has published several war poems. He is the first American to receive an honorary degree at Oxford since the United States entered the war. The degree of Doctor of Civil Law was conferred upon him on May 8, 1917.

VERNÈDE, ROBERT ERNEST. He was educated at St. Paul's School and at St. John's College, Oxford. On leaving college he became a professional writer, producing several novels and two books of travel sketches, one dealing with India, the other with Canada. He was also author of a number of poems. At the outbreak of the war he enlisted in the Nineteenth Royal Fusiliers, known as the Public Schools Battalion, and received a commission as Second Lieutenant in the Rifle Brigade, in May, 1915. He went to France in November, 1915, and was wounded during the battle of the Somme in September of the following year, but returned to the front in December. He died of wounds on April 9, 1917, in his forty-second year.

WATERHOUSE, GILBERT. Lieutenant in the Second Essex Regiment. His war writings include *Railhead, and other Poems*. He is reported "missing."

WHARTON, EDITH. She has written *Fighting France*, etc.

INDEX OF FIRST LINES

O gracious ones, we bless your name
O living pictures of the dead
O race that Caesar knew
Of all my dreams by night and day
Often I think of you, Jimmy Doane
Oh, down by the Millwall Basin as I went the other day
Oh, red is the English rose
Oh! yon hills are filled with sunlight, and the green leaves paled to gold
Our little hour,—how swift it flies
Out where the line of battle cleaves
Over the twilight field

Qui vive? Who passes by up there?
Quiet thou didst stand at thine appointed place

Robbed mother of the stricken Motherland

Saints have adored the lofty soul of you
See you that stretch of shell-torn mud spotted with pools of mire
Shadow by shadow, stripped for fight
She came not into the Presence as a martyred saint might come
She was binding the wounds of her enemies when they came
Shyly expectant, gazing up at Her
Sometimes I fly at dawn above the sea

The battery grides and jingles
The falling rain is music overhead
The first to climb the parapet
The horror-haunted Belgian plains riven by shot and shell
The naked earth is warm with Spring
The road that runs up to Messines
The starshells float above, the bayonets glisten
There are five men in the moonlight
There is a hill in England
There is wild water from the north
They had hot scent across the spumy sea

They sent him back to her. The letter came
This is my faith, and my mind's heritage
This is the ballad of Langemarck
This was the gleam then that lured from far
Those who have stood for thy cause when the dark was around thee
Thou warden of the western gate, above Manhattan Bay
Thou, whose deep ways are in the sea
Three hundred thousand men, but not enough
To the Judge of Right and Wrong
'T was in the piping time of peace

Under our curtain of fire
Under the tow-path past the barges
Unflinching hero, watchful to foresee

Was there love once? I have forgotten her
We are here in a wood of little beeches
We challenged Death. He threw with weighted dice
We may not know how fared your soul before
We willed it not. We have not lived in hate
What have I given
What is the gift we have given thee, Sister?
What of the faith and fire within us
What was it kept you so long, brave German submersible?
When battles were fought
When consciousness came back, he found he lay
When first I saw you in the curious street
When the fire sinks in the grate, and night has bent
When there is Peace our land no more
Whence not unmoved I see the nations form
Wherever war, with its red woes
With arrows on their quarters and with numbers on their hoofs
With proud thanksgiving, a mother for her children

Ye sleepers, who will sing you
You dare to say with perjured lips
You have become a forge of snow-white fire

Made in the USA